W9-ABI-390

TECHNICAL COLLEGE OF THE LOWCOUNTRY
LEARNING RESOURCES CENTER
POST OFFICE BOX 1288
BEAUFORT, SOUTH CAROLINA 29901-1288

Modern Critical Interpretations

Thomas Hardy's
Jude the Obscure

Modern Critical Interpretations

These and other titles in preparation

Thomas Hardy's
Jude the Obscure

Edited and with an introduction by
Harold Bloom
Sterling Professor of the Humanities
Yale University

Chelsea House Publishers
NEW YORK ◊ PHILADELPHIA

TECHNICAL COLLEGE OF THE LOWCOUNTRY,
LEARNING RESOURCES CENTER
POST OFFICE BOX 1288
BEAUFORT, SOUTH CAROLINA 29901-1288

© 1987 by Chelsea House Publishers, a division
of Main Line Book Co.

Introduction © 1987 by Harold Bloom

All rights reserved. No part of this publication may be
reproduced or transmitted in any form or by any means
without the written permission of the publisher.

Printed and bound in the United States of America

10 9 8 7 6 5 4 3 2

∞ The paper used in this publication meets the minimum
requirements of the American National Standard for
Permanence of Paper for Printed Library Materials,
Z39.48–1984.

Library of Congress Cataloging-in-Publication Data
Thomas Hardy's Jude the obscure.
   (Modern critical interpretations)
   Bibliography: p.
   Includes index.
   Summary: A collection of eight critical essays on
Thomas Hardy's last major novel, arranged in
chronological order of publication.
   1. Hardy, Thomas, 1840–1928. Jude the obscure.
[1. Hardy, Thomas, 1840–1928. Jude the obscure.
2. English literature—History and criticism] I. Bloom,
Harold. II. Series.
PR4746.T48 1986   823'.8   86–18883
ISBN 0–87754–741–6

Contents

Editor's Note

This book gathers together a representative selection of the best criticism of Thomas Hardy's last major novel, *Jude the Obscure*. The essays are reprinted here in the chronological order of their original publication. I am grateful to Jennifer Wagner for her erudition and judgment in helping me to edit this volume.

My introduction sets *Jude the Obscure* in the context of a tragic tradition that moves from Schopenhauer and Shelley through Hardy and D. H. Lawrence. The chronological sequence of criticism begins with Michael Millgate's biographical study of the novel, and then continues with Janet Burstein's account of *Jude*'s relation to a postmythic cosmos that has forsaken the comforts of a mythical story of origins.

Ian Gregor positions *Jude* in Hardy's literary career, while Terry Eagleton's Marxist exegesis provides a social perspective that is clearly useful, though Hardy would have rejected it. In a brief but telling analysis, Norman Page emphasizes both the strength of Jude's visual insights, and the blindness to reality caused by Jude's sexual drive and by his childish over-idealization of the university as a kind of earthly Jerusalem.

Kathleen Blake, studying the feminism of Sue Bridehead, concludes that "Sue's breakdown is not a judgment on her," but rather "a judgment on the way things are between the sexes," at least in Hardy's vision. Current theories of "the reader's share" in any literary text are applied to *Jude* by Ramón Saldívar, who discovers in the novel a stance of rhetorical self-consciousness in which the prose is on the verge of passing over into Hardy's later poetry.

This book ends with Philip M. Weinstein's analysis of Jude's complex fate, in which Jude is held to be not an innocent Job, but "obscurely complicit in his own downfall," while always being unable to locate and name the nature of that ironic complicity.

Introduction

For Arthur Schopenhauer, the Will to Live was the true thing-in-itself, not an interpretation but a rapacious, active, universal, and ultimately indifferent drive or desire. Schopenhauer's great work, *The World as Will and Representation,* had the same relation to and influence upon many of the principal nineteenth- and early twentieth-century novelists that Freud's writings have in regard to many of this century's later, crucial masters of prose fiction. Zola, Maupassant, Turgenev, and Tolstoy join Thomas Hardy as Schopenhauer's nineteenth-century heirs, in a tradition that goes on through Proust, Conrad, and Thomas Mann to culminate in aspects of Borges and Beckett, the two most eminent living writers of narrative. Since Schopenhauer (despite Freud's denials) was one of Freud's prime precursors, one could argue that aspects of Freud's influence upon writers simply carry on from Schopenhauer's previous effect. Manifestly, the relation of Schopenhauer to Hardy is different in both kind and degree from the larger sense in which Schopenhauer was Freud's forerunner or Wittgenstein's. A poet-novelist like Hardy turns to a rhetorical speculator like Schopenhauer only because he finds something in his own temperament and sensibility confirmed and strengthened, and not at all as Lucretius turned to Epicurus, or as Whitman was inspired by Emerson.

The true precursor for Hardy was Shelley, whose visionary skepticism permeates the novels as well as the poems and *The Dynasts.* There is some technical debt to George Eliot in the early novels, but Hardy in his depths was little more moved by her than by Wilkie Collins, from whom he also learned elements of craft. Shelley's tragic sense of eros is pervasive throughout Hardy, and ultimately determines Hardy's understanding of his strongest heroines: Bathsheba Everdene, Eustacia Vye,

1

Marty South, Tess Durbeyfield, Sue Bridehead. Between desire and fulfillment in Shelley falls the shadow of the selfhood, a shadow that makes love and what might be called the means of love quite irreconcilable. What M. D. Zabel named as "the aesthetic of incongruity" in Hardy and ascribed to temperamental causes is in a profound way the result of attempting to transmute the procedures of *The Revolt of Islam* and *Epipsychidion* into the supposedly naturalistic novel.

J. Hillis Miller, when he worked more in the mode of a critic of consciousness like Georges Poulet than in the deconstruction of Paul de Man and Jacques Derrida, saw the fate of love in Hardy as being darkened always by a shadow cast by the lover's consciousness itself. Hugh Kenner, with a distaste for Hardy akin to (and perhaps derived from) T. S. Eliot's in *After Strange Gods,* suggested that Miller had created a kind of Proustian Hardy, who turns out to be a case rather than an artist. Hardy was certainly not an artist comparable to Henry James (who dismissed him as a mere imitator of George Eliot) or James Joyce, but the High Modernist shibboleths for testing the novel have now waned considerably, except for a few surviving high priests of Modernism like Kenner. A better guide to Hardy's permanent strength as a novelist was his heir D. H. Lawrence, whose *Rainbow* and *Women in Love* marvelously brought Hardy's legacy to an apotheosis. Lawrence, praising Hardy with a rebel son's ambivalence, associated him with Tolstoy as a tragic writer:

> And this is the quality Hardy shares with the great writers, Shakespeare or Sophocles or Tolstoi, this setting behind the small action of his protagonists the terrific action of unfathomed nature; setting a smaller system of morality, the one grasped and formulated by the human consciousness within the vast, uncomprehended and incomprehensible morality of nature or of life itself, surpassing human consciousness. The difference is, that whereas in Shakespeare or Sophocles the greater, uncomprehended morality, or fate, is actively transgressed and gives active punishment, in Hardy and Tolstoi the lesser, human morality, the mechanical system is actively transgressed, and holds, and punishes the protagonist, whilst the greater morality is only passively, negatively transgressed, it is represented merely as being present in background, in scenery, not taking any active part, having no direct connexion with the protagonist. Œdipus, Hamlet, Macbeth set themselves up against, or find themselves set up against, the un-

fathomed moral forces of nature, and out of this unfathomed force comes their death. Whereas Anna Karenina, Eustacia, Tess, Sue, and Jude find themselves up against the established system of human government and morality, they cannot detach themselves, and are brought down. Their real tragedy is that they are unfaithful to the greater unwritten morality, which would have bidden Anna Karenina be patient and wait until she, by virtue of greater right, could take what she needed from society; would have bidden Vronsky detach himself from the system, become an individual, creating a new colony of morality with Anna; would have bidden Eustacia fight Clym for his own soul, and Tess take and claim her Angel, since she had the greater light; would have bidden Jude and Sue endure for very honour's sake, since one must bide by the best that one has known, and not succumb to the lesser good.

("Study of Thomas Hardy")

This seems to me powerful and just, because it catches what is most surprising and enduring in Hardy's novels—the sublime stature and aesthetic dignity of his crucial protagonists—while exposing also his great limitation, his denial of freedom to his best personages. Lawrence's prescription for what would have saved Eustacia and Clym, Tess and Angel, Sue and Jude, is perhaps not as persuasive. He speaks of them as though they were Gudrun and Gerald, and thus have failed to be Ursula and Birkin. It is Hardy's genius that they are what they had to be: as imperfect as their creator and his vision, as impure as his language and his plotting, and finally painful and memorable to us:

> Note that, in this bitterness, delight,
> Since the imperfect is so hot in us,
> Lies in flawed words and stubborn sounds.

II

Alone among Hardy's novels, *Jude the Obscure* has three strong figures, all triumphs of representation: Sue, Jude, Arabella. Unfortunately, it also has little Father Time, Hardy's most memorable disaster in representation. Even more unfortunately, it is a book in which Hardy's drive to go on telling stories gives way to his precursor Shelley's despair that there is one story and one story only, the triumph of life over human integrity. As the most Shelleyan of Hardy's novels (except perhaps for *The Well-Beloved,* which precedes it in initial composition, though not in revision and publication), *Jude the Obscure* has a complex and perhaps crippling relation to *Epipsychidion.* Sue Bridehead is more Shelleyan than even Shelley's Emilia in that poem, and would have been better off married to Shelley than to Jude Fawley, which is not to say that poor Shelley could have survived the union any better than the unhappy Jude.

D. H. Lawrence, inevitably, was Sue's most articulate critic:

> Her female spirit did not wed with the male spirit: she could not prophesy. Her spirit submitted to the male spirit, owned the priority of the male spirit, wished to become the male spirit.

Sue needs no defense, least of all in 1986 when she has become prevalent, a subtle rebel against any dialectic of power founded wholly upon mere gender. Yet, within the novel, Sue is less a rebel than she is Jude's Shelleyan epipsyche, his twin sister (actually his cousin) and counterpart. She can live neither with Jude, nor without him, and their love is both narcissistic and incestuous, Hardy's metaphor for the Will to Live at its most destructive, because in Jude and Sue it destroys the most transcendent beings Hardy had ever imagined.

It will not suffice to call *Jude the Obscure* a tragedy, since what is most tragic in Jude and Sue is their Shelleyan transcendence. When Shelley attempted tragedy in *The Cenci,* he succeeded only by diverting the form into a lament for the descent of Beatrice Cenci to her father's level. But Jude and Sue cannot be said to descend, any more than Eustacia, Henchard, and Tess descend. The Will to Live in Hardy's cosmos is too terrible and too incessant for us to speak of it as debasing its subjects or victims. In a world dominated by drive, a spirit like Jude's is condemned to die whispering the Jobean lament: "Let the day perish wherein I was born." *Jude the Obscure* is Hardy's Book of Job, and like Job is too dark for tragedy, while unlike Job it is just the reverse of theodicy, being Hardy's ultimate declaration that the ways of the Immanent Will towards man are unjustifiable.

Few interchanges in literature are at once so pathetic and so charming as the intricate, Shelleyan dances of scruple and desire intertwined that involve Sue and Jude:

> He laughed. "Never mind," he said. "So that I am near you,
> I am comparatively happy. It is more than this earthly wretch

called Me deserves—you spirit, you disembodied creature, you dear, sweet, tantalizing phantom—hardly flesh at all; so that when I put my arms round you, I almost expect them to pass through you as through air! Forgive me for being gross, as you call it! Remember that our calling ourselves cousins when really strangers was a snare. The enmity of our parents gave a piquancy to you in my eyes that was intenser ever than the novelty of ordinary new acquaintance."

"Say those pretty lines, then, from Shelley's 'Epipsychidion' as if they meant me," she solicited, slanting up closer to him as they stood. "Don't you know them?"

"I know hardly any poetry," he replied, mournfully.

"Don't you? These are some of them:

> "'There was a Being whom my spirit oft
> Met on its visioned wanderings far aloft.
>
> .   .   .   .
>
> A seraph of Heaven, too gentle to be human,
> Veiling beneath that radiant form of woman . . .'"

"Oh, it is too flattering, so I won't go on! But say it's me!—say it's me!"

"It *is* you, dear; exactly like you!"

"Now I forgive you! And you shall kiss me just once there—not very long." She put the tip of her finger gingerly to her cheek, and he did as commanded. "You do care for me very much, don't you, in spite of my not—you know?"

"Yes, sweet!" he said, with a sigh, and bade her goodnight.

It is Sue, right enough, and it is disaster. The true epigraph to *Jude the Obscure* comes at the climax of *Epipsychidion*:

> In one another's substance finding food,
> Like flames too pure and light and unimbued
> To nourish their bright lives with baser prey,
> Which point to Heaven and cannot pass away:
> One hope within two wills, one will beneath
> Two overshadowing minds, one life, one death,
> One Heaven, one Hell, one immortality,
> And one annihilation.

That "one will beneath" the "two overshadowing minds" of Sue and Jude is the Immanent Will of Thomas Hardy, and it indeed does become "one annihilation."

The Tragedy of Unfulfilled Aims

Michael Millgate

In the 1912 postscript to the original preface [to *Jude the Obscure*] Hardy observed that the theme of the marriage that had become "a cruelty" to one of the parties, and hence "essentially and morally no marriage," had "seemed a good foundation for the fable of a tragedy, told for its own sake as a presentation of particulars containing a good deal that was universal, and not without a hope that certain cathartic, Aristotelian qualities might be found therein." Within the novel itself, Sue speaks at one point of a "tragic doom" overhanging the Fawleys "as it did the house of Atreus," and it becomes clear that Hardy is again deliberately invoking, as earlier in *The Return of the Native,* images, analogies, and even structural patterns derived ultimately from Greek drama. Aunt Drusilla and the Widow Edlin have something of the role of a chorus; Jude quotes from the *Antigone* and from the *Agamemnon;* the book ends with a prophecy by Arabella—"She's never found peace since she left his arms, and never will again till she's as he is now!"—which seems strikingly similar to the famous conclusion of *Oedipus Tyrannus,* rendered, in the translation which Hardy used, as "call no man happy, ere he shall have crossed the boundary of life, the sufferer of nought painful." If it seems excessive to suggest that in calling Jude "the Obscure" Hardy may have had in mind an ironic allusion to such titles as Oedipus "the King," it is at least conceivable that in writing *Jude* he had the career of Oedipus very much in mind.

From *Thomas Hardy: His Career as a Novelist.* © 1971 by Michael Millgate. Random House, 1971.

The introduction to the translation of Sophocles which Hardy owned praised *Oedipus Rex* as "the most complicated and artfully sustained of extant Greek plays," one in which "we are continually kept in alternate doubt, fear, and hope." In the highly self-conscious patterning of *Jude* the steadily downward curve of the tragedy is repeatedly delayed or disguised by moments of "alternate doubt, fear, and hope," even as its inexorability is repeatedly confirmed by instances of inversion, reversal, and *peripeteia*—seen at its bitterest in the outcome of Jude's last visit to Sue. The apparently excessive suffering of Jude and Sue in the final chapters has caused difficulty to readers and critics alike, and has perhaps cast a kind of retrospective pall over earlier novels of Hardy's in which the outcome is in fact much less desperate and unrelieved. Edmund Gosse voiced such feelings in his review of *Jude* in the *St James's Gazette:*

> It is a very gloomy, it is even a grimy, story that Mr. Hardy has at last presented to his admirers. . . . We do not presume to blame him for the tone he has chosen to adopt, nor for the sordid phases of failure through which he drags us. The genius of this writer is too widely acknowledged to permit us to question his right to take us into what scenes he pleases; but, of course, we are at liberty to say whether we enjoy them or no. Plainly, we do not enjoy them. We think the fortunes, even of the poorest, are more variegated with pleasures, or at least with alleviations, than Mr. Hardy chooses to admit. . . . But in his new book Mr. Hardy concentrates his observation on the sordid and painful side of life and nature. We rise from the perusal of it stunned with a sense of the hollowness of existence.

This represents a kind of charge against Hardy, and specifically against *Jude,* which it is perhaps impossible to refute as completely as one might wish. There does seem to be something gratuitous about Jude's sufferings, the death of Father Time and the other children, the violence of Sue's abnegation and self-flagellation. In view, however, of the Greek precedents Hardy seems to have had in mind, such turns of the screw can perhaps be explained, if not entirely justified, in terms of a deliberate determination to leave the reader precisely "stunned with a sense of the hollowness of existence."

Hardy responded warmly to Gosse's review in a series of letters on which Gosse drew, in turn, in writing a second and more extended review of the novel for the first issue of the international literary journal, *Cosmopolis*. That some of Gosse's remarks rankled, however, is clear from the postscript to the first of these letters:

> One thing I did not answer. The "grimy" features of the story go to show the contrast between the ideal life a man wished to lead, and the squalid real life he was fated to lead. The throwing of the pizzle, at the supreme moment of his young dream, is to sharply initiate this contrast. But I must have lamentably failed, as I feel I have, if this requires explanation and is not self-evident. The idea was meant to run all through the novel. It is, in fact, to be discovered in *everybody's* life, though it lies less on the surface perhaps than it does in my poor puppet's.

What Gosse so gratingly characterised as the "grimy" episodes in *Jude* were crucial to Hardy's whole conception, though it is significant of Hardy's sensitivity to criticism even at this late stage of his career that in revising the novel in 1903 he should have reduced the explicitness of Jude's first encounter with Arabella—a scene deplored, of course, by other reviewers besides Gosse himself.

But if his revision removed the visual grotesquerie of Jude and Arabella engaging in amorous dalliance with the pig's pizzle dangling between them, Hardy retained a strong comic element in the scene, introducing, for example, a reference to Arabella's "novel artillery." To the schoolroom battle at Shaston, another scene to which objection had been made when the book first appeared, Hardy in his 1912 revision for the Wessex Edition added the farcical detail of the church warden being "dealt such a topper with the map of Palestine that his head went right through Samaria." Such scenes, Hardy had observed to Gosse on November 20, 1895, might more appropriately be compared to Fielding, to whom he himself "felt akin locally," than to Zola, in whom he was "very little" read, and there seems no doubt that he saw them as primarily comic both in form and function.

One remarkable feature of *Jude* is the lightness of the opening manner: the early pages offer few hints of the way the story is to end. If the tone here is scarcely comic, it is often humorous, and Jude himself tends to be viewed with affectionate amusement. While we may sympathise with his compassion for the birds he is supposed to be scaring away, we also smile at his lack of practical good sense. His entrapment into marriage is a disaster, but the tricks used by Arabella Donn (that arable bella donna) are of a kind which would, in a slightly different context, make Jude into a butt for time-honoured mirth. Comic irony is everywhere implicit in the vanity of Jude's ambitions, a soaring superstructure based on frail foundations; in his manner of listing the vast undone as if, somehow, it was as good as accomplished; in the disruption of this train of thought by the arrival of Arabella's outrageous missile. The first hint of interruption coincides with the mention of Aristophanes in the recital of authors he has yet to read; the pizzle itself arrives just as he has made a virtual godhead of Christminster and a Christ of himself: "Yes, Christminster shall be my Alma Mater; and I'll be her beloved son, in whom she shall be well pleased."

The irony, emphatic yet controlled, serves several purposes. Not only is the relative lightness at the beginning a necessary starting point for the story's subsequent decline into disaster and death, but the occasional presentation of Jude in a humorous light helps to establish a sense of his normality, his human fallibility, and thus to prevent his appearing as an offensive prig. The juxtaposition of Jude's dogged Anglicanism with Sue's frank paganism—his assumption, for example, that Miss Fontover must have destroyed Sue's statues because they were "too Catholic-apostolic for her"—is one of several ways in which the note of comedy is kept alive, and with it our sense of Jude as a potentially comic figure. The commentary provided by Aunt Drusilla and the Widow Edlin also incorporates comic elements, while even Phillotson, in his moment of abnegation, is made to cut a ludicrous figure in the world's eyes and given a central role in the outright comedy of the brawl at the public enquiry.

As the example of Phillotson would suggest, the alternation of "doubt, fear, and hope" runs throughout the novel. Although the course of events is persistently downward, the descent into utter disaster following the fatal return to Christminster in pursuit of Jude's obsession is both late and sudden. Only a few chapters earlier, in the scene at the Great Wessex Agricultural Show, Jude and Sue have been seen at their happiest, and the positive aspects of their comradeship have received their strongest celebration:

> Sue, in her new summer clothes, flexible and light as a bird, her little thumb stuck up by the stem of her white cotton sunshade, went along as if she hardly touched ground, and as if a moderately strong puff of wind would float her over the hedge into the next field. Jude, in his light grey holiday-suit,

was really proud of her companionship, not more for her external attractiveness than for her sympathetic words and ways. That complete mutual understanding, in which every glance and movement was as effectual as speech for conveying intelligence between them, made them almost the two parts of a single whole.

The momentary upward movement is skilfully held in check by the looming background presence of a scornful yet envious Arabella, appearing here, as so often in the novel, as a figure of ill omen. If the promise of what might yet be is strong, so is the blighting threat of what must be.

The pattern of *Jude* cannot be spoken of as a fall from "great estate," except in so far as the central figure does exemplify—in all aspects of his emotional, intellectual, and spiritual life—the gradual, relentless atrophy of hope, the one thing in which he had been rich when the novel opened. Hardy spoke in his original preface of "the tragedy of unfulfilled aims," and if this is understood as applying not merely to the educational theme but to the whole of Jude's experience it sufficiently points to the degree of waste and agony involved. It is, indeed, tempting to reflect on the possible association of Jude's name with that of Judas Iscariot, and on the theme of betrayal as it appears in the novel. Jude in the latter stages of the book speaks of himself, in self-dramatising fashion, as Sue's "seducer," but if he technically betrays Sue, this is far outweighed by her eventual betrayal of their achieved relationship when she returns to Phillotson, who himself betrays by his final surrender to selfishness and repressiveness the altruism and open-mindedness he had originally shown in letting Sue go. Jude's most serious betrayal is surely of his own dream, as he abandons the pursuit of education and self-advancement at the first contact with Arabella's sexuality, while dominating the whole book is the sense of Christminster's betrayal of Jude, his efforts, and his ambitions.

This larger treachery has itself to be evaluated in terms of our cumulative awareness of the ultimate self-betrayal of Christminster itself and, by implication, of the society and civilisation of which it is the fine flower. As the book proceeds, it becomes increasingly clear not merely that Christminster is impregnable to such as Jude, but that the values the college walls protect are themselves hypocritical and debased. The point is heavily underlined by the incident in which the cab-driver kicks his horse in the belly: "'If that can be done,' said Jude, 'at college gates in the most religious and educational city in the world, what shall we say as to how far we've got?'" Christminster, though "religious and educational," is not enlightened. Jude on his first visit to the city had recalled the enthusiastic words of Matthew Arnold:

> "Beautiful city! so venerable, so lovely, so unravaged by the fierce intellectual life of our century, so serene! . . . Her ineffable charm keeps ever calling us to the true goal of all of us, to the ideal, to perfection."

Although Jude, Hardy notes, had forgotten that Arnold also "mourned Christminster as 'the home of lost causes,'" his subsequent experiences conspire to teach him that what Christminster represents and teaches is far from synonymous with sweetness and light. Yet the fascination with Christminster remains, as obsessive, as illusory, and, for Jude and those dear to him, as dangerous as Sue's rigid adherence to shifting principles and her propensity for "impulsive penances." The dream gains the upper hand, indeed, just at the moment when human and economic needs are greatest, becoming a nightmare as Jude insists on watching the Remembrance Day procession, ignoring both the rain which is to lead eventually to his own death and the lack of lodgings which is to lead immediately to the death of his children.

Ultimately, perhaps, Jude's obsession with Christminster should be seen in terms of its relationship to deeper, obscurer needs. What he carves on the milestone is not "Christminster" but "Thither." Hardy at one point suggests that Jude's obsession goes absolutely against the grain of his background, his training, and his own best instincts. When Jude first seeks work in Christminster he goes to a busy stone-mason's yard:

> For a moment there fell on Jude a true illumination; that here in the stone yard was a centre of effort as worthy as that dignified by the name of scholarly study within the noblest of the colleges. But he lost it under stress of his old idea. He would accept any employment which might be offered him on the strength of his late employer's recommendation; but he would accept it as a provisional thing only. This was his form of the modern vice of unrest.

Hardy places a high value on Jude's skill, and on the dignity of craftsmanship; he also establishes here the ironies implicit in Jude's quest, in his rejection of that valuable possession his craftsmanship for the sake of a false grail. Clearly, there is a bitter sense in which the Master of Biblioll

College is right to advise Jude that the best chances of success lie in "remaining in your own sphere and sticking to your trade." Characteristically, however, Hardy undercuts this position by pointing out that the work being done in the yard was "at best only copying, patching and imitating," and that the mediaevalism in which Jude (like Hardy himself) had been trained was "as dead as a fern-leaf in a lump of coal." The paragraph quoted nonetheless illustrates Hardy's skill in drawing out and sustaining all the ironies implicit in his material and in his story, and in manipulating the occupation of his protagonist as an element integral to the total pattern. It is not simply that Hardy uses developments in architectural decoration to suggest much broader historical movements, or that the craftsmanship involved in stone-masonry is established as an alternative ideal to the one which Jude actually pursues; even more important is the way in which Jude's trade is one which ties him to old buildings, churches, and graveyards—to the restoration of the past and the perpetuation of precisely those influences and traditions which bar his educational and social aspirations and menace the privacy of his life with Sue. Jude and Sue are necessarily at war with dogma, with regulations, with rules of conduct, and their dismissal from the task of restoring the lettering of the Ten Commandments develops into a kind of savage pun on the novel's epigraph, "The letter killeth."

The allusive device is entirely characteristic of a novel in which points are driven home with the firmness and almost the explicitness of the marginal commentary in the *Pilgrim's Progress*. For none of the characters in *Jude* does Hardy offer anything approaching an extended psychological analysis: his people are made to reveal themselves in action and in dialogue. Even fundamentally unreflective characters like Arabella are required to indulge in verbalised self-analysis, and the novel moves through a series of moments not so much of vision as of revelation, with the central characters defining their mingled affinity and opposition through direct intellectual or emotional confrontation, or in terms of their differing responses to people, objects, or institutions wholly external to themselves and their immediate relationship. So Jude and Arabella clash over the killing of the pig, Jude and Sue disagree over Christminster and react differently to the pictures at Wardour Castle:

> They reached the Park and Castle and wandered through the picture-galleries, Jude stopping by preference in front of the devotional pictures by Del Sarto, Guido Reni, Spagnoletto, Sassoferrato, Carlo Dolci, and others. Sue paused patiently

beside him, and stole critical looks into his face as, regarding the Virgins, Holy Families, and Saints, it grew reverent and abstracted. When she had thoroughly estimated him at this, she would move on and wait for him before a Lely or Reynolds. It was evident that her cousin deeply interested her, as one might be interested in a man puzzling out his way along a labyrinth from which one had one's self escaped.

As so often in Hardy, the points of external reference are not merely concrete but authentic. Wardour Castle, an actual place, contained just such paintings as Hardy specifies. Similarly, Shaston is the old name for Shaftesbury, and the town is described in phrases taken in part from Hutchins's *History and Antiquities of Dorset*. To all intents and purposes Christminster *is* Oxford, Melchester Salisbury. *Jude* is crowded with place-names, often thinly disguised adaptations of the real names of substantial towns in and near the Thames Valley—places, that is to say, well-known to many of his readers, not remote Dorset hamlets but precisely the kind of "raw towns that we believe and die in." Movement from place to place is persistent throughout the novel, its importance emphasised by the heading given to the various parts: "At Marygreen," "At Christminster," and so on. Yet *Jude* is a novel curiously deficient in the sense of place. Apart from Christminster and Shaston, the places visited by Sue and Jude remain, by comparison with the places in Hardy's other novels, singularly devoid of individuality, atmosphere, associations. Gosse, in his *Cosmopolis* review, attributed this to the quality of the actual landscape:

> Berkshire is an unpoetical county, "meanly utilitarian," as Mr. Hardy confesses; the imagination hates its concave, loamy cornfields and dreary, hedgeless highways. The local history has been singularly tampered with in Berkshire; it is useless to speak to us of ancient records where the past is all obliterated, and the thatched and dormered houses replaced by modern cottages. In choosing North Wessex as the scene of a novel Mr. Hardy wilfully deprives himself of a great element of his strength. Where there are no prehistoric monuments, no ancient buildings, no mossed and immemorial woodlands, he is Sampson shorn. In Berkshire, the change which is coming over England so rapidly, the resignation of the old dreamy elements of beauty, has proceeded further than anywhere else in Wessex. Pastoral loveliness is to be discovered only here

and there, while in Dorsetshire it still remains the master-element.

The criticism is an unwitting acknowledgment of Hardy's success. Like the prophecies, the sudden violent events, and the clamorous ironies, the multiple settings of *Jude* serve to throw into relief at once the sequence and the patterning of the central action. The story is full of arrivals and departures, new beginnings attempted and old paths inadvertently re-entered. The featureless towns and villages of North Wessex—Aldbrickham, Stoke-*Barehills*, and the rest—answer precisely to the rootlessness of the nomadic life to which Jude and Sue are progressively reduced. They also perhaps serve, like the stages of Tess's pilgrimage, as Bunyanesque testing-places of the soul and as externalisations of internal states. W. J. Keith has argued, indeed, that the landscape of the novel is in effect the creation of Jude's own vision and intellect and functions less as background or setting than as "symbolic commentary."

The narrative itself follows these journeyings with unusual closeness. Instead of moving all aspects of the story forward concurrently, at more or less the same pace, Hardy tends to push ahead quickly on a narrow front, following the history of a particular character or group of characters and leaving other contemporary aspects of the story to be covered at a later stage. Thus we are kept, with Jude, in ignorance of Arabella's return from Australia until she suddenly materialises behind the bar in Christminster. When Sue leaves Phillotson we find she has gone to meet Jude by previous arrangement, though there had been no firm indication of this before her departure. At the simplest, of course, this method brings to the narrative an element of surprise and even of suspense. More generally, and perhaps more importantly, it contributes to the experience of restlessness and discontinuity, to the way in which good intentions are unexpectedly thwarted, ideals abruptly shattered, the best-laid plans turned suddenly awry.

The characteristic restlessness of the novel operates as an image, a dramatic reflection, of "the modern vice of unrest." Hardy apparently comprehends in this term not only the breakdown in traditional patterns of rural life and the greater ease of physical mobility brought about by those railways which play such an important part in *Jude,* but also the spiritual and intellectual disruption of the time, Matthew Arnold's "strange disease of modern life." Jude is perhaps in some sense ironically identified with the hero of "The Scholar-Gypsy," whom the narrator—himself seated on a hill-top, whence his eye, like Jude's from the Brown

TECHNICAL COLLEGE OF THE LOWCOUNTRY
LEARNING RESOURCES CENTER
POST OFFICE BOX 1288
BEAUFORT, SOUTH CAROLINA 29901-1288

House, "travels down to Oxford's towers"—imagines as wandering in solitude, cherishing "the unconquerable hope" with a tenacity impossible to a more sophisticated world. The urgent warning to the Scholar-Gypsy embodies a prediction which closely matches Jude's own case:

> "But fly our paths, our feverish contact fly!
>   For strong the infection of our mental strife,
>   Which, though it gives no bliss, yet spoils for rest;
>   And we should win thee from thy own fair life,
>   Like us distracted, and like us unblest,
>   Soon, soon thy cheer would die,
>   Thy hopes grow timorous, and unfix'd thy powers,
>   And thy clear aims be cross and shifting made;
>   And then thy glad perennial youth would fade,
>   Fade, and grow old at last, and die like ours."

Jude does not escape the infection. Christminster beckons him; the echoes of the Tractarian movement have reached even his little village; neither his faith nor Sue's unbelief proves sufficient to withstand the strains put upon them. As in *The Return of the Native* and *A Laodicean,* both of which anticipate important aspects of *Jude,* there are suggestions of a deliberate rejection of Arnoldian ideas. No more than in those earlier novels, however, does Hardy offer a resolution of the intellectual and social dilemmas which his characters confront. "Like former productions of this pen," observes the 1895 preface, "*Jude the Obscure* is simply an endeavour to give shape and coherence to a series of seemings, or personal impressions, the question of their consistency or their discordance, of their permanence or their transitoriness, being regarded as not of the first moment." If the intellectual concepts embodied in *Jude* do not cohere, that is perhaps because they were never intended to do so, because Hardy conceived and composed his last novel as a comprehensive image of intellectual and social chaos. If the wandering Jude is permitted visions of a promised land, he is himself forbidden to enter it, and Hardy closes the book—and, with it, his career as a novelist—on a scene of despair, bitterness and death, of mankind still languishing in the wilderness. Hardy can scarcely have expected such a novel to be universally welcomed, and the crucial paragraph of his original preface not only summarised the book's central themes and hinted at their relative importance but sounded an unmistakable note of conscious challenge:

For a novel addressed by a man to men and women of full

age; which attempts to deal unaffectedly with the fret and fever, derision and disaster, that may press in the wake of the strongest passion known to humanity; to tell, without a mincing of words, of a deadly war waged between flesh and spirit; and to point the tragedy of unfulfilled aims, I am not aware that there is anything in the handling to which exception can be taken.

The Journey beyond Myth in *Jude the Obscure*

Janet Burstein

In *Jude the Obscure* one confronts an image, quite familiar to the modern reader, of the single self grown beyond its dimly remembered union with the natural and social world. *Jude* was not the first of Thomas Hardy's works to represent the self thus, in isolation from its world, nor was Hardy the only Victorian writer concerned with this problem. In his conclusion to *The Renaissance* (1873; rpt. London, 1910), for example, Walter Pater wrote that

> if we continue to dwell in thought on this world . . . the whole scope of observation is dwarfed into the narrow chamber of the individual mind. Experience, already reduced to a group of impressions, is ringed round for each one of us by that thick wall of personality through which no real voice has ever pierced on its way to us, or from us to that which we can only conjecture to be without. Every one of those impressions is the impression of the individual in his isolation, each mind keeping as a solitary prisoner its own dream of a world.

The individual's capacity to dream his "own dream of a world" may have been celebrated without much qualification earlier in the century, but some Victorian writers, as Pater's essay suggests, associated the development of consciousness and personal vision with the isolation and imprisonment of the self.

Isolated individuals figure in all of Hardy's later fiction, and their

From *Texas Studies in Literature and Language* 15, no. 3 (Fall 1973). © 1973 by the University of Texas Press.

suffering is often contrasted with the more stable lives of men for whom a coherent community still exists. Thus Hardy's work characteristically juxtaposes two modes of perceiving and experiencing life in the world: a modern way in which self-consciousness yields its dubious rewards, and an older way that might be called "mythic." The juxtaposition is artistically effective, for it clarifies peculiarities of each way, and offers to characters within the world of the novels the illusion of choice. Michael Henchard, for example, falls back upon the folk way when he consults the weather seer; and Tess returns to the way of her ancestors when she murders d'Urberville.

This characteristic pattern also exists in *Jude the Obscure*. But although Hardy's last novel is again "all contrasts," it seems to deny both the possibility of "choice" and the viability of a return to an older or mythic way. The first section of this study will approach that apparent denial by setting Hardy's sense of myth in a limited nineteenth-century context. The second section will deal more closely with the novel itself, and will suggest that in *Jude* Hardy rejected the notion of a fruitful return to a mythic way of knowing the experiential world and explored instead the problems of the human journey beyond myth.

The term "mythic" seems appropriate to the world of Hardy's rustics, for it explains, to some extent, the attractiveness of that world to characters like Tess and Henchard. As many nineteenth-century readers knew, myths originated among men who had not yet differentiated themselves from their natural and social worlds; myths, therefore, were understood to express a fundamental coherence of man and world, and to represent a better integrated perception of the world than the self-conscious modern mind could achieve. Moreover, as myth seemed to be the voice of a community in which shared understandings of the world were articulated, it offered the memory of communal support to characters like Tess and Henchard who had grown apart from the ways of their kind.

Insights such as these into the nature and function of myth were not uncommon in the literature of the century. Karl Otfried Müller, whose *Introduction to a Scientific System of Mythology* was published in English translation in 1844 (trans. John Leitch, London), held that myth spoke of both the inner, subjective world of ideality and the objective world of fact. George Grote (*History of Greece,* I [1846; rpt. New York, 1849]) also believed that myth represented an integrated and coherent perception of the world which proceeded from the "instinctive tendencies of the feeling and imagination to transport, to the world without, the familiar type of free will and conscious personal action." Both historians recognized that the perceptions represented in myths were held in common by communities of men: myth derived, Müller said, from an oral and popular tradition and originated with a certain "necessity and unconsciousness" among men; and Grote spoke of the Homeric myths as being adapted "to the universal sympathies and hearty interest of a crowd of hearers."

Historians and other, more strictly literary, students of myth were impressed by its "suggestive way of regarding the universe as a spiritual whole, and man in relation to it as a part thereof." Walter Pater noticed that even postmythic Greek sculpture represented a human "connexion with earth and air . . . direct and immediate; in precise contrast to our physical theory of our life" (*Greek Studies* [1895; rpt. London, 1967]). This "sympathy between the ways and aspects of outward nature and the moods of men" (*Greek Studies*) seems to have been particularly beguiling to Victorian minds, for the nostalgia for an older mode of rapprochement between man and Nature exists in much of the literature of the century.

Hardy recognized in this "sympathy" between man and Nature the anthropomorphizing tendency of the mythic mind. He saw in William Barnes's "peasant" an "absolute dependence on the moods of the air, earth and sky," which was conducive to a mythic perception of nature: "Sun, rain, wind, snow, dawn, darkness, mist, are to him, now as ever, personal assistants and obstructors, masters and acquaintances, with whom he comes directly into contact, whose varying tempers must be well-considered before he can act with effect." Hardy perceived this mythically anthropomorphizing tendency of thought in himself as well: "In spite of myself," he wrote, "I cannot help noticing countenances and tempers in objects of scenery, e.g. trees, hills, houses."

However, although Hardy seems to have shared an understanding of myth common in this period, he seems also to have been ambivalent about the value of myth as a way of perceiving one's world. On one hand, he understood mythic perception to be both characteristic of an earlier stage of human development and essential to all poetic vision:

> Mr. E. Clodd this morning gives an excellently neat answer
> to my question why the superstitions of a remote Asiatic and
> a Dorset labourer are the same: "The attitude of man," he
> says, "at corresponding levels of culture, before like phenomena, is pretty much the same, your Dorset peasants repre-

senting the persistence of the barbaric idea which confuses persons and things, and founds wide generalizations on the slenderest analogies." (This "barbaric idea which confuses persons and things" is, by the way, also common to the highest imaginative genius—that of the poet.)

(*The Early Life of Thomas Hardy*)

Hardy later justified the poetic value of this "barbaric idea" by alluding to his own use of it in *Tess:* it was, he wrote, a "well known trope explained in that venerable work, *Campbell's Philosophy of Rhetoric,* as 'one in which life, perception, design, passion, or any property of sentient beings is attributed to things inanimate.'" But on the other hand, he declared it part of his own perceptual attitude "in spite of" himself and described it as a "semi-madness, which sees enemies, etc., in inanimate objects."

This ambivalence towards myth as a mode of perception distinguishes Hardy's attitude sharply from Pater's, for Pater often stressed the need of the modern mind to return to a mythic mode: he spoke of this need in cultural rather than in individual terms in *The Renaissance* where he suggested that modern culture would benefit from being "drawn back to its sources" for clarification and correction. Indeed, Pater often pointed to aspects of Greek thought and art that seemed to offer a wholesome corrective to modern tendencies: he cited the saturation of concrete sensual form with human meaning in Greek art as a model of coherence, and the inclusiveness of Greek religion as a model of spiritual wholeness. Contemplating the Hellenic ideal "in which man is at unity with himself, with his physical nature, with the outward world," Pater was inclined to "regret" man's need to grow beyond that ideal. And in the later studies of Dionysus and Demeter, Pater returned to the study of myth itself, rather than its representation in art, to show the chief virtue of mythic imagination: a "unifying or identifying power" which the modern mind, he believed, had lost (*Greek Studies*).

The wistfulness of Pater's work may derive from his endless regret that such imaginative power may indeed have been lost to modern men. In *Tess of the D'Urbervilles* and *The Mayor of Casterbridge* Hardy also appears, at times, to betray authorial regret over the loss of myth as a satisfactory way of knowing. But *Jude the Obscure* faces that loss and seems to accept it as final. Jude's world, as many readers have noticed, is like our own; and the perceptual and conceptual peculiarities that fragment Jude's experience and isolate him from other men are heavily underlined by the recognition, implicit in the novel, that the illusory hope of a potentially fruitful return to myth has disappeared.

From the beginning, *Jude the Obscure* confronts one with a fictional world scarred by its enforced separation from the age of myth. In contrast to the mythic world, which was distinguished chiefly by the harmony and coherence of its features, Jude's world seems tragically disfigured by a lack of coherence, and by the many losses it has sustained in its passage through time. Among these losses one notes first the disappearance of human meaning from the landscape of the novel, for the natural world so rich in associations for the mythic mind has been quite emptied of meaning for young Jude. Of all the relics of "local history" at Marygreen, the well-shaft alone remains "absolutely unchanged." It discloses a "shining disc of quivering water at a distance of a hundred feet down. There was a lining of green moss near the top, and nearer still the hart's tongue fern." This image offers the life-giving qualities of fresh water as a "counterweight" to the arid sterility of other natural phenomena in *Jude;* the well is represented as the single remnant of a vital past in the natural world of the novel, for most other such remnants have been erased.

Jude speaks the human response to such a world: "'How ugly it is here,'" he murmurs, as he observes the large concave field in which he works. But the narrator supplies an insight deeper than Jude's into the reason for the ugliness: fresh harrow lines, he says, lent "a meanly utilitarian air to the expanse, taking away its gradations and depriving it of all history beyond that of the few recent months, though to every clod and stone there really attached associations enough and to spare—echoes of songs from ancient harvest-days, of spoken words, and of sturdy deeds." One notes that the narrator assumes a function here that he performs throughout the novel: his is actually the only voice left to speak the richness of a vanished life and time; only his eyes perceive the dimensions of the past which round out the flat, dull features of the world in *Jude* and give them density and meaning.

A reader comes to depend upon this narrative voice, for until it speaks the events of the plot seem to lack a dimension; the narrator's voice orients one in time and enriches one's experience of the novel by making the past eloquent. Conversely, characters within the novel who hear no voices like the narrator's seem curiously adrift in time and lost in a world where phenomena may have many contradictory meanings—

or none at all. Thus Hardy emphasizes the impoverishment of such characters' experiences in a postmythic world by juxtaposing Jude's perception of Troutham's Field, for example, with the narrator's.

But the novel does not suggest that memory like the narrator's would offer a way of restoring meaning to Jude's world for those who live within it. The narrator may remember roads and pathways once important and now forgotten, but he sees too that such roads are largely obsolete. "There is in Upper Wessex," he says,

> an old town of nine or ten thousand souls; the town may be called Stoke-Barehills. . . . The great western highway from London passes through it, near a point where the road branches into two, merely to unite again some twenty miles further westward. Out of this bifurcation and reunion there used to arise among wheeled travelers, before railway days, endless questions of choice between the respective ways. But the question now is as dead as the scot-and-lot freeholder, the road waggoner, and the mail coachman who disputed it; and probably not a single inhabitant of Stoke-Barehills is now even aware that the two roads which part in his town ever meet again.

Memory serves here to draw from the past an image of the divisions and separations that disfigure the world of the novel; and memory links the fact of "bifurcation" with the promise of "reunion." But the "railway" has superseded this road; memory cannot restore it to usefulness, for the uses of the past have been outgrown.

One could see in this description of the single road that divides and meets again a wonderfully apt image of the growth of human consciousness and the corresponding changes in the world perceived by men, for as men grow beyond the myth in which all aspects of self and world are fused, the world itself may seem to change; indeed, as consciousness moves towards the differentiation of self from world and of "myself" from other selves, the natural and social world may begin to manifest "divisions" actually taking place within the human mind. "Division" is, to be sure, an important fact of Jude's world; the narrative begins on a note of division—Phillotson's departure from Marygreen—and proceeds to the "split" that divided Sue's parents from each other and the "changes" that have separated Marygreen from its human past. Christminster and Marygreen folk have always maintained the strictest separation, Aunt Fawley says; and Jude is soon made aware of a "flaw in the terrestrial scheme" that differentiates men from birds. The first chapter thus announces the theme of division in several areas of human life: the separation of teacher from pupil, of present from past, of parents from children (Jude is an orphan, one remembers) and from each other, of townsmen from countrymen, and of men from other creatures. Such divisions seem to be part of the "given" of Jude's world; they are the human facts of life beyond the point where the road divides, and the mythic coherence of man and world gives way to the differentiation of self and the growth of personal vision.

But the promise of "reunion" offered by the image of the divided road seems to have become as obsolete as the road itself, for traditional agents of reconciliation are no longer effective. Language, for example, which may have brought men together in the past, now seems to deepen rather than to heal the divisions between them. Jude and Sue are continually frustrated by the failure of words to bridge the separation that divides them from each other; their conversations are both fascinating and bewildering, for the great burden of their thought and feeling is rarely articulated. When they arrive at the inn, for example, and Sue questions Jude about his previous meeting there with Arabella, Jude admits he "can't explain" this encounter. Sue cries:

> "O don't you understand my feeling! *Why* don't you! Why
> are you so gross! *I* jumped out of the window!"
> "Jumped out of the window?"
> "I can't explain."
> ". . . you don't understand me either. Women never do!

Jude turns to a generalization about women because the feelings of this woman are, like his own, unsayable. Thus he seems to have been defeated here, as elsewhere in the novel, by language.

Sue's peculiarly capricious verbal behavior suggests that she too senses the inadequacy of language. At times she is evasive, turning conversation away from important subjects. At other times she uses language defensively, talking "incessantly" of unimportant things "as if she dreaded his indulgence in reflection." Like Jude, who abjures explanation altogether and determines to "keep silence" in some cases, she is also capable of suppressing speech. It seems ironically appropriate that Sue's spoken words to Father Time unleash the catastrophe that ensues, for her verbal behavior seems "capricious" only if one overlooks the potentially destructive failure of language in this novel to help individuals understand each other.

Instead of nurturing human relationships by illuminating personal insights that may be generally valid, language in a postmythic world seems chiefly to reflect the disparity between individual and general or conventional perceptions. Phillotson acknowledges the discrepancy between his own use of language and the general usage when he says wryly that he has been asked to resign "on account of my scandalous conduct in giving my tortured wife her liberty—or, as they call it, 'condoning her adultery.'" And Jude makes a similar discrimination between "their" use of language and his own: when Sue suggests that she and Jude are, in fact, "'living together,'" Jude replies, "'Yes. But not in their sense.'"

The remote legal jargon of the divorce papers and the archaic wording of the marriage contract suggest both the inappropriateness and the superficiality of conventional language. More significantly, these documents suggest the grim consequences that threaten individuals when language regulates, but does not faithfully represent, individual experience in the world. Jude speaks his awareness of those consequences when he says, twice, that Sue "'does not realize what marriage means!'" And Phillotson, when he has learned the meaning of that word, tells his disapproving friend: "'I don't think you are in a position to give an opinion. I have been that man, and it makes all the difference in the world.'" The warning offered at the beginning and repeated close to the end of the novel—"the letter killeth"—suggests that words may actually be inimical to human life when they have ceased to articulate the deep truth of individual experience.

Like the natural world, then, from which past associations have disappeared, the world of men in *Jude* has been impoverished by a loss of meaning in conventional language. And in neither case does recollection of earlier meanings or associations relieve the consequent deprivation of characters in the novel: Christminster's illustrious past cannot be brought into any helpful relationship to Jude, and the Widow Edlin's recollection of what "marriage" meant in her own time is quite irrelevant to Sue and Jude and Phillotson, who cannot find in the Widow's memories the value of that word to their own experience. Thus the novel seems to distinguish between artistic and other uses of the past, much as Hardy distinguished the poet's use of myth from its more questionable effect upon his own way of seeing. The narrator's memory offsets the deficiencies of landscape and language for the reader; but memory fails to restore meaning—either to natural phenomena or to words—for characters within the novel itself.

The failure of language and memory, moreover, is echoed by other failures in *Jude* which may be associated with what we have called the obsolescence of old ways, or Hardy's denial of the virtue of return. Jude's indecisive returnings to the Fourways in Christminster, his dogged study of dead languages, Phillotson's study of Roman antiquities, and Sue's passion for pagan statuary are all failures in that they do not afford any usable insights into existential problems. Jude's work in stone may also be seen as a symbolic return manqué, for its object is "regenerative" not creative. The old ways and words in *Jude,* like the Gothic buildings he seeks to restore, have not only fallen into disrepair; their efficacy has been destroyed by the "deadly animosity of contemporary logic," and they simply do not work anymore. Antique houses, as Sue puts it, are "'very well to visit but not to live in.'"

Thus all the characters in *Jude* seem to live at a point beyond the "bifurcation" of the road, and although memory of an older, more coherent way persists, people find no living traces of it in their world, nor, sadly, any promise that former human values will be restored. In their rootless uncertainty they resemble the "proprietors of wandering vans, shows, shooting galleries and other itinerant concerns" who constitute a peculiar feature, "this a modern one," of the landscape at Shaston:

> As strange wild birds are seen assembled on some lofty promontory, meditatively pausing for longer flights, or to return by the course they followed thither, so here, in this cliff-town, stood in stultified silence the yellow and green caravans bearing names not local, as if surprised by a change in the landscape so violent as to hinder their further progress; and here they usually remained all the winter till they turned to seek again their old tracks in the following spring.

Like the owners of those caravans, some characters in *Jude* also wish to return to "old tracks," but those who attempt to return find the way back to be as perilous, now, as the way ahead.

Initially, return to an older, more mythic way is complicated by those "change[s] in the landscape" that disfigure the world of the novel and frustrate "further progress." But an even more formidable barrier to return is presented by changes that have occurred within human consciousness itself. Sue, for example, has acquired a way of knowing and of looking at the world that ensures a detachment quite alien to the mythic mind. Sue avoids a mythic immersion in experience and seeks instead to see her world within the firmly established and painstakingly maintained confines of the separate self; the window motif associated with Sue throughout the novel suggests that she is identified with a way of seeing that functions satisfactorily *only* within a frame. She talks more comfortably with Jude when there is a window frame between them; and her many notes to Jude, as well as her exchange of notes with Phillotson, may indicate that she is less fearful of the word when it is fixed on a page. Sue's delight in the roses exhibited at the fair might also be seen in light of her dependence on frames: as she avoids confronting Jude's feeling or her own because, "seeing it more than he, [she] would not allow herself to feel it," she seems also to avoid confronting the feelings stirred by lovely things in their natural context; the roses at the fair, one remembers, have been cut out of context for exhibition and wait passively to be admired and "named."

Frames may allow Sue to control the chaos of impressions experienced by the modern, self-conscious mind, "ringed round," as Pater put it, "by that thick wall of personality"; but Sue's control is, at best, precarious; her detachment is threatened both by her husband's assertion of his conjugal rights and by the boarding school's assertion of conventional standards. And her way of seeing seems to make it impossible for her to deal with such threats: in both instances she retreats precipitately through windows. These two jumps, and the number of doors she tries to tie or lock shut, suggest that in her case detachment has ripened into alienation. She has become, like Pater's "solitary prisoner," incapable of moving outward from the self to deal with the world beyond. Indeed, she is unable to proceed through doorways or even to open one herself: when she rescues her pigeons she merely pulls out the peg of the cage door, trusting the birds to open it themselves; and in her final interview with Phillotson she hovers helplessly between the closed doors of her bedroom and his.

Sue's "progress" is clearly "hindered," then, by her way of seeing and of being in the world, as well as by the nature of the world she experiences. And her return is similarly obstructed. Though she seeks to reenter an older, more mythic coherence of man and world, she remains imprisoned within the frame of the self. The narrator describes her attempted return as an "exchange" in which reason yields to anthropomorphism: after the children's funeral, he reports, Jude and Sue sit

> silent, more bodeful of the direct antagonism of things than
> of their insensate and stolid obstructiveness. Vague and quaint
> imaginings had haunted Sue in the days when her intellect

scintillated like a star, that the world resembled a stanza or melody composed in a dream; it was wonderfully excellent to the half-aroused intelligence, but hopelessly absurd at the full waking; that the First Cause worked automatically like a somnambulist, and not reflectively like a sage; that at the framing of the terrestrial conditions there seemed never to have been contemplated such a development of emotional perceptiveness among the creatures subject to those conditions as that reached by thinking and educated humanity. But affliction makes opposing forces loom anthropomorphous; and those ideas were now exchanged for a sense of Jude and herself fleeing from a persecutor.

Sue exchanges sophisticated and highly individualistic "ideas" here for an old convention that rests upon naïve belief, rather than reason:

> "We must conform!" she said mournfully. "All the ancient wrath of the Power above us has been vented upon us, His poor creatures, and we must submit. There is no choice. We must. It is no use fighting against God!"

But the exchange is quite fruitless. The comforts of embracing an "anthropomorphous" God who acts upon his creatures and orders their experience are denied to Sue by her awareness, never wholly repressed, that no such God exists. Moreover, her submission does not alleviate her alienation; on the contrary, she remains convinced that the world is unalterably hostile. She wishes to "satisfy the world which does not see things as they are" because she cannot conceive a genuine reconciliation of "their" world and her own; thus, her submission affirms her weakness but preserves her separateness. One notes that the dramatic consequences of Sue's return to anthropomorphism justify Hardy's ambivalence about myth as a way of knowing and expose the dangers latent in nostalgia for a mythic way.

Phillotson's development reveals still another problem inherent in the notion of return. He does not abandon reason for belief; he seeks instead to replace principle with instinct, to "exchange" the rules that govern human relationships in a civilized world for the unconscious and instinctive fellow feeling that may have provided social coherence in a mythic world.

Phillotson is "'only a feeler'" he says, "'not a reasoner,'" and when first he acts by "'instinct, and let[s] principles take care of themselves'" his feeling for Sue allows him to release her from an untenable contract. Like Jude's feeling for the hungry birds, this instinct is obviously benign. But human feeling cannot be relied upon, it seems, to work sympathetically in all situations; Phillotson's treatment of Sue at the novel's end, still motivated by feeling, is no longer kind, but incredibly cruel. The narrator explains:

> Principles which could be subverted by feeling in one direction were liable to the same catastrophe in another. The instincts which had allowed him to give Sue her liberty now enabled him to regard her as none the worse for her life with Jude. He wished for her still, in his curious way, if he did not love her, and, apart from policy, soon felt that he would be gratified to have her again as his, always provided that she came willingly.

Clearly, neither the subversion of principle by instinct nor the exchange of reason for anthropomorphic belief accomplishes a fruitful return. The comfortably coherent world once conceived by the mythic mind, and dimly remembered by modern men, seems inaccessible now; one cannot reenter it by way of belief in its Gods, nor can one restore it by abjuring principles and reinstating a "magic thread of fellow feeling" as a basis for human relationships. Neither human belief nor human sympathy seems to have survived the passage through time intact; both have been qualified by the development of self-centeredness and personal vision.

These developments in human consciousness are most explicitly dealt with in Jude himself, for Jude's self-absorption and the limitations it imposes upon his perception of the world are obvious throughout the novel. Indeed, Jude's subjective manipulation of the objective world seems almost deliberate at times: the narrator says that although Jude "knew well, too well, in the secret center of his brain, that Arabella was not worth a great deal as a specimen of woman kind. . . . For his own soothing he kept up a factitious belief in her. His idea of her was the thing of most consequence, not Arabella herself, he sometimes said laconically."

Jude also fashions other experiential phenomena nearer to his own desire: in Christminster

> when he passed objects out of harmony with [the city's] general expression he allowed his eyes to slip over them as if he

did not see them. A bell began clanging, and he listened till
a hundred and one strokes had sounded. He must have made
a mistake, he thought: it was meant for a hundred.

When the phenomenological world evades the form he projects onto it,
Jude adjusts the evidence of his senses to make it accord with his personal
vision.

The narrator's description of Jude's childhood suggests that this
perceptual and conceptual maneuvering may be linked to the growth of
human consciousness in time. As young Jude works in Troutham's Field
he experiences a peculiarly mythic, or childlike, sense of harmony with
the world: a "magic thread of fellow feeling united his life" with the
feeding birds, and he grants them their food though it is not his to
grant. His punishment separates him sharply from this way of seeing:
whirled round by the angry farmer, he sees "the hill, the rick, the plan-
tation, the path, and the rooks going round and round him in an amaz-
ing circular race."

Jude weeps afterward, from shame, and feels "more than ever his
existence to be an undemanded one." And when he reflects upon the
experience, he conceives the shame and pain and disharmony in "Nature's scheme," which prevents hungry birds from feeding and boys
from feeling wanted, as inevitable aspects of growing up:

> Events did not quite rhyme as he had thought. Nature's logic
> was too horrid for him to care for. That mercy towards one
> set of creatures was cruelty towards another sickened his sense
> of harmony. As you got older, and felt yourself to be at the
> center of your time, and not at a point in its circumference,
> as you had felt when you were little, you were seized with a
> sort of shuddering, he perceived. All around you there seemed
> to be something glaring, garish, rattling, and the noises and
> glares hit upon the little cell called your life, and shook it,
> and warped it.
>
> If he could only prevent himself growing up! He did not
> want to be a man.

Jude's growth in this episode might serve as a metaphor for the growth
of human consciousness beyond the mythic stage, for they have in common the separation of the human being from the natural world with
which he once identified himself (in the birds), the loss of community

(his life is "undemanded"), and the emergent sense of self as both distinct from and central to its world.

One must pause on the last point, however, for it speaks a misapprehension of the episode as one sees it from the narrator's point of view. Jude's perception of himself as central to a whirling, "glaring, garish, rattling" world is understandable in his circumstances, but it is clearly inaccurate. Though he sees himself fixed in the center of an agitated world, he is actually being whirled round within a world vastly more stable, at the moment, than he. And his initial perceptual error is deepened and fixed by further reflection. He associates growth not only with the differentiation of self and world, but also with the notion of self as central to its world; thus he projects a new relationship or "harmony" quite feasible from a subjective point of view, but sadly inappropriate to the objective reality of his situation.

In short, Jude moves beyond the "bifurcation" of the road, and the loss of mythic coherence, into the cell of the self where the reciprocal development of man and world ultimately ceases. For Hardy, however, an end to such mutual development was inconceivable. His personal writings reveal that he was, on the contrary, deeply committed to continued evolutionary growth. Hardy recognized the "woeful fact that the human race is too extremely developed for its corporeal conditions, the nerves being evolved to an activity abnormal in such an environment." Nevertheless, he seems to have believed that despite the "woeful facts" given to perception by the post-mythic world, human consciousness must continue to evolve: "the visible signs of mental and emotional life," he wrote, "must like all other things keep moving, becoming." Hardy knew the pain of evolution: "It is the ongoing—i.e. the 'becoming'—of the world," he wrote, "that produces its sadness." But he appears to have believed that that sadness was an inescapable fact of the human condition in his time.

Thus, although the novel presents "sadness" as a fact of contemporary life, Jude's maturing responses may also present an image of the way men might learn both to grow beyond myth and to endure the sadness that accompanies such growth. Symbolically, Jude's way, like Sue's, is identified with doors and windows—but his perspective is significantly wider, more open than hers. His view from the barn roof at the Brown House in Marygreen is dominated, to be sure, by a single object of desire, but by the time he ascends to the many windowed "octagonal chamber" in Christminster he commands a succession of views and is able to place himself quite realistically within the wide world he now perceives.

Unlike Sue, who appears to withdraw to the security of framed and shuttered windows, Jude seems to proceed vigorously through the successive doorways presented to him by his experience. He is able to look at the world in Christminster "meditatively, mournfully, yet sturdily" because he has begun to learn to live with the sadness of becoming. His first response to early trauma was, as we have noted, quite negative: having substituted the isolated unit of the self for the outgrown unity of self and world, Jude wished he could "prevent himself growing up. He did not want to become a man." His second disappointment is more easily borne: although the Latin and Greek textbooks shatter a "grand delusion," Jude recovers: "in the course of a month or two after the receipt of the books Jude had grown callous to the shabby trick played him by the dead languages"; indeed, "to acquire languages, departed or living, in spite of such obstacles as he now knew them inherently to possess, was a herculean performance which gradually led him on to a greater interest in it."

Similarly, although he attempts suicide just after his quarrel with Arabella, he later accepts his situation with almost philosophic calm: "'I am a man,' he said. 'I have a wife. More, I have arrived at the still riper stage of having disagreed with her, disliked her, had a scuffle with her, and parted from her.'" And his realistic assessment is succeeded by a new resolution: "Surely his plan should be to move onward through good and ill—to avoid morbid sorrow even though he did see uglinesses in the world . . . to do good cheerfully—which he had heard to be the philosophy of one Spinoza, might be his own even now."

One notes that although Jude's "progress" is "hindered" it is not, like Sue's, wholly obstructed. Jude does not seem to be immobilized by the cruelties of experience; he grows beyond them. And he remains deeply involved in the stuff of his life even as he acquires the perspective necessary to endure that involvement. Unlike both Sue and Phillotson, he holds to the reality of personal, self-conscious experience while he learns to abandon self-centeredness and to perceive himself in a larger context. Though he outgrows the notion of self as central to its world, he acquires a sense of himself as vital, and related to the world of other men.

In some respects the world of men seems, in this novel, to have replaced the personal God once believed to have shaped the universe for man's education and delight. Jude alludes to such a replacement in the novel, and the substitution accords with Hardy's thinking, as one sees it in his journal. Preoccupied with the disappearance of a personal God, he wrote:

> I have been looking for God fifty years, and I think that if he existed I should have discovered him. As an external personality, of course—the only true meaning of the word.

But three months later, concerned with what was left to men when the "anthropomorphous" Deity accessible to the mythic mind had disappeared, Hardy wrote:

> Altruism, or the Golden Rule, or whatever "Love your neighbor as yourself" may be called, will ultimately be brought about I think by the pain we see in others reacting on ourselves, as if we and they were a part of one body. Mankind, in fact, may be and possibly will be viewed as members of one corporeal frame.

The world of men in *Jude* is hardly like the "one corporeal frame" envisioned by Hardy in this passage, but the novel does suggest that this may be a new "harmony" to be sought by those who would journey beyond myth.

Indeed, despite Jude's often painful singularity, he may approach such a conception of harmony, for he begins to perceive a relationship between himself and other men. He attempts to describe this new perception to Sue:

> "I have seemed to myself lately . . . to belong to that vast band of men shunned by the virtuous—the men called seducers. It amazes me when I think of it! I have not been conscious of it, or of any wrongdoing towards you, whom I love more than myself. Yet I *am* one of those men! I wonder if any other of them were the same purblind, simple creatures as I? . . . Yes, Sue—that's what I am. I seduced you. . . . you were a distinct type—a refined creature intended by Nature to be left intact. But I couldn't leave you alone!"

Jude's insight, drawn from deeply personal experience, is extended in this passage to the "vast band of men" called seducers; and the extension both relates Jude to others like himself and fills the word "seducer" with new meaning. Thus Jude seems to participate here in solving a fundamental problem of the postmythic world; perhaps language, like an ancient wine cup richly engraved with vineleaves—yet empty—must be replenished with the truth of personal experience if it is to satisfy human need and work against individual isolation.

Jude recognizes the need as well for a corresponding re-creation of value, based upon personal experience, in the conventions that create and govern social coherence in a postmythic world. In words that evoke the memory of Pater's Marius, Jude describes his "present rule of life" to the crowd at Christminster. Like Marius, who reassured himself that he had done no man harm, Jude says: "'I doubt if I have anything more for my present life than following inclinations which do me and nobody else any harm, and actually give pleasure to those I love best.'" But his next words extend this limited concern with self and loved ones into the world of other men: "'I perceive,'" Jude says, "'there is something wrong somewhere in our social formulas: what it is can only be discovered by men or women with greater insight than mine,—if, indeed, they ever discover it—at least in our time.'" As one critic has noticed, Marius's philosophy was restrictive: "he cannot act, cannot mingle, cannot read his time right or guide it." Jude suffers some of the same limitations, but he moves beyond Marius insofar as he asserts that the inadequacy of "social formulas" affects him and that "insight" must relate those formulas to the facts of personal experience.

Finally, it seems fitting that although Jude dies with Job's curse on his lips the responsive voice of God is silent, and one hears instead the raucous noises of an ignorant multitude. The scene images both the disappearance of a personal God and the undeniable disharmony in Jude's world—the cruel absence of coherence among men. But this scene also presents an image of the way in which such coherence might be recreated, for the partly opened window allows "their" voices to enter Jude's room, and to furnish there a human context for his last despairing words.

Thus the novel offers no panacea for despair in a postmythic world, nor any hope of returning to the more comfortable world of myth. It offers instead the somewhat baffled quest of sensitive and vulnerable individuals for a way of relating themselves again to a world both ignorant of and indifferent to their needs. And it suggests as well that the relationship they seek will rest upon their ability to penetrate the isolation of self-centered personal vision—to open windows rather than withdraw behind them. Jude fumbles toward such a goal throughout the novel, and his openness and growing enlightenment may redeem, to some extent, his many failures. One is depressed by those failures, one supposes, because Jude's journey is so painful, and so obscure. But Hardy offers no consolation other than Jude's confidence in the "essential soundness" of his way and the suggestion that, like Jude's dream of going to college, the reconciliation of man and world is a goal to be sought through many generations by those who journey beyond myth.

An End and a Beginning:
Jude the Obscure

Ian Gregor

More than any other of his novels Hardy's last work draws our attention to the form it takes. Hardy realised this and in a characteristically depreciatory and laconic remark observed about *Jude:* "The book is all contrasts—or was meant to be in its original conception. Alas, what a miserable accomplishment it is, when I compare it with what I meant to make it!—e.g. Sue and her heathen gods set against Jude's reading the Greek testament; Christminster academical, Christminster in the slums; Jude the saint, Jude the sinner; Sue the pagan, Sue the saint; marriage, no marriage; etc. etc."

From such a description we might well conclude that "form" was a very external thing for Hardy, a self-conscious designing into effective shape of material already present to his imagination. But our sense of the form of the novel in reading it, is of something much more turbulent, a sense not of imposed design but of vexed movement, as if Hardy, in leaving the Wessex novels behind him, had mined a new power within himself, but a power no longer always under his own control. If the novel is "all contrasts," this is indicative of the way in which the tension which I have described as a central element in the substance of the Wessex novels has now worked its way into the very structure of his fiction. In the chapter that follows I would like to argue that in *Jude* we see Hardy driving his fiction to its furthest extreme, and discovering as he does so, new territories for himself, but territories which only a later kind of fiction will be able to explore satisfactorily.

From *The Great Web: The Form of Hardy's Major Fiction.* © 1974 by Ian Gregor. Faber & Faber, 1974.

Perhaps the most obvious sign which indicates the variety of pressures at work in the novel is the difficulty we have in saying, however baldly, just what the novel is "about." It seems, almost ostentatiously, to be "about" so many things—a malevolent universe, an outworn system of education, the rigidity of the marriage laws, or, as one of its most recent critics has put it, "the sheer difficulty of human beings living elbow to elbow and heart to heart; the difficulty of being unable to bear prolonged isolation or prolonged closeness; the difficulty, at least for reflective men, of getting through the unspoken miseries of daily life." There is no reason why a novel should not be about all these things and achieve its own formal unity—but in the case of *Jude* we do feel a genuine disparateness of theme, a constant oscillation of interests. The total effect the novel makes is of massive coherence, a coherence arising less, however, from the substance of the book than from its mood and tone.

We can put the matter in more historical terms. From one point of view we feel that *Jude* is the work of a man for whom the universe makes—or ought to make—rational sense; it is something "out there" to be interrogated, pondered over. And the interrogator, though he may be sceptical in his enquiry, frustrated and disappointed by his conclusions, is never in doubt about the validity or the importance of his undertaking. An entry in Hardy's journal for January 1890 catches the mood: "I have been looking for God for 50 years, and I think that if he had existed I should have discovered him. As an external personality, of course—the only true meaning of the word." It is the note of a detective in search of a Missing Person, confident that nothing has been overlooked and with no doubt as to the "true meaning" of clues. But it is not the particulars of Hardy's scepticism that make us think of *Jude* as a nineteenth-century novel, so much as the more generalised feeling that the novelist, with all his assurances and doubts, hopes and fears, is present in his work in a very direct way, and yet in a way which quite forbids us to confuse fiction with autobiography. There is a grandeur of conception, a completeness of commitment, a quality of caring, which has all been transmuted into art, and yet which we feel impelled to describe in personal terms; for the integrity of the art has about it a transparency which makes the integrity of the artist an inseparable part of our reading experience. With this kind of fiction before us we have no difficulty in understanding the positive quality there might be in the description "the novelist as sage." Nevertheless, it is this element which marks out *Jude* as not of our own time, and of course it is a quality which extends into every detail of the fiction.

Within this firm and articulated structure, however, there glimmers another kind of novel which could only be described in terms very different from these we have been using. Far from the characters in *Jude* seeming fixed, they are seen in constantly shifting emphases and depths, taking themselves—and us—by surprise; the plot is less a narrative line made up of interlocking events, than a series of significant but isolated moments: the ideas debated seem integral to the characters rather than on loan from the author. Though the novel is structured in terms of places, they hardly seem to matter, and as the characters move restlessly from one place to another, the world of the novel seems to be less in Wessex than at the nerves' end. Above all, the novel is conceived in terms of rhythm, markedly seen in the elaborate contrasting and counterpointing of character and incident, but even more significantly felt in the rhythm of the whole, where in the evolving relationship of section to section, the central themes gradually reveal themselves. If *Jude* prompts us to think of "the novelist as sage," it prompts us no less to think of "the novel as process," and with that description we think of the fiction of our own time, with its multiplicity of techniques, its interior landscapes, its careful irresolutions.

Implicit in this dualistic impression which the novel makes is a tension, but unlike the tension present in the Wessex novels, it is now present in the very form the novel takes. From one point of view, it is quite clear that in *Jude* Hardy wanted to evoke a sense of cosmic tragedy, with a novel claiming epic status; from another point of view, however, that is by no means so clear, if we see it, not in its compositional totality, but as an unfolding process. Here the sources of the tragedy are more complex, the ironies more subtle, the tone more wry and more detached.

In the pages that follow I would like to argue that the power of Hardy's last singular achievement was shaped by a conflict between a kind of fiction which he had exhausted and a kind of fiction which instinctively he discerned as meeting his need, but which, imaginatively, he had no access to.

II

There occurs an incident in Jude's boyhood which both focuses this duality of emphasis and provides an image which serves to introduce a reading of the novel as a whole. Jude, pursuing his dream of learning, has sent to Christminster for some Greek and Latin grammars:

Ever since his first ecstasy or vision of Christminster and its possibilities, Jude had meditated much and curiously on the probable sort of process that was involved in turning the expressions of one language into those of another. He concluded that a grammar of the required tongue would contain, primarily, a rule, prescription, or clue of the nature of a secret cipher, which, once known, would enable him, by merely applying it, to change at will all words of his own speech into those of the foreign one . . . He learnt for the first time that there was no law of transmutation, as in his innocence he had supposed.

"He learnt for the first time that there was no law of transmutation"—this is a lesson which is to preoccupy Hardy, no less than Jude, as the novel develops. The language in which men seek to make clear to themselves their metaphysical questions, their educational needs, their emotional longings, is in constant need of interpretation. One idiom must be found to complement another. To feel as Jude does that here is some "secret cipher, which, once known, would enable him, by merely applying it" to master his problem, is a dangerous illusion—whether that illusion finds expression in the prophesyings of Aunt Drusilla, the cynical pragmatism of Arabella, or the fervent idealism of Sue. The incident of the grammars initiates Jude into a life-long education in which he is to learn that there is no simple law of transmutation by which one kind of experience can be simply translated into another, there is only "a series of seemings"—a phrase which directs us both to the manner and the matter of his novel.

One of the most remarkable things about *Jude* is the tone of the first part—"At Marygreen." It is a tone intimately related to the pace of the narrative, uncomfortably reminiscent at times of early silent films. At the still centre is Jude—lying in a field looking through the interstices of his straw hat at "something glaring, garish, rattling, and the noises and glares hit upon the little cell called your life, and shook it, and warped it." "Events did not rhyme quite as he thought"—that sentence could well stand as an epigraph for the section as a whole. Unlike the Wessex novels, which generally build up gradually, *Jude* plunges us directly into tragedy, or at least the potentialities of tragedy, *con brio*. From the opening pages, Aunt Drusilla reminds us of Jude's luckless existence, "It would ha' been a blessing if Goddy-mighty had took thee too, wi' thy mother and father, poor useless boy"; we have Jude deserted by Phillotson, his only friend, thrown out of his job by Farmer Troutham, deceived by Vilbert—so that long before he has even met Arabella he has felt "his existence to be an undemanded one," and indeed wished "that he had never been born." The second half of this opening section drives home these feelings without pause—he meets Arabella at the point when his self-education is beginning to take shape, she tricks him into marriage, they have a brutally short and cynical life together, and then she leaves him. We are hardly surprised that Jude—knowing him as we do—walks out to the centre of a frozen pond and seeks to drown himself. From the moment of his arrival at his aunt's house, orphaned and alone, to the moment when Arabella deserts him some seven or eight years later, he would hardly seem to have known more than the most fleeting moments of happiness. Looked at simply in the light of events and the speed with which they succeed each other, the whole opening section is so relentless that it operates dangerously near the area of black farce.

And yet, as we read, it does not strike us in this way. The reason is not far to seek. It is because we find in Jude, playing directly against the force of these events, an instinctive resilience: "Like the natural boy, he forgot his despondency, and sprang up"—that too is the note struck by the first section, and if the background contains the Clytemnestra-like tones of Aunt Drusilla, there is also the persistent glow of Christminster on the distant horizon with its promise of a life elsewhere. Perhaps what is so striking about the Marygreen section of the novel is the way in which everything is pushed to extremes—the ugliness of the immediate scene contrasted with the city of light glimpsed through the surrounding mists, Jude's absorption with the birds and the clout from the Farmer, and most of all, the juxtaposition of Jude's dream of learning "Livy, Tacitus, Herodotus, Aeschylus, Sophocles, Aristophanes—" with the sounds on the other side of the hedge, "Ha, ha, ha! Hoity-toity!" What is interesting to note however is that, while the substance of this first section may not seem uncharacteristic of Hardy, it is all accelerated in such a way that the impression it makes is laconic, faintly offhand, as if Hardy feels that these extremities of tragedy and unfocused aspiration are much too simple a rendering of experience. "Events did not rhyme as he had thought," this theme is to be caught again and again in the novel, but in a way which makes us increasingly aware that the apocalyptic tones of the opening will become subdued, as Christminster transforms itself from "a glow in the sky," an ideal to be lived for, into buildings, streets, people.

"It was a windy, whispering, moonless night. To guide himself he opened under a lamp a map he had brought"—and so Jude begins his exploration of Christminster. His first encounter is not with the present of Christminster, but with its past; and as he wanders through the deserted streets in the moonless night he hears the voice of the university in the accents of Addison, Gibbon, Peel, Newman and, most clearly, in Arnold's famous apostrophe, "Beautiful city! so venerable, so lovely, so unravaged by the fierce intellectual life of our century, so serene!" The clash intimated by Arnold, between the serenity of Oxford and its remoteness from contemporary intellectual concern, foreshadows the stance to be taken by Sue and indeed it is ironically caught in Jude's first glimpse of her at work in the Anglican bookshop—"A sweet, saintly, Christian business, hers"—while her thoughts dwell on the pagan deities she has bought to decorate her room and the books of Gibbon and Mill which provide her nightly reading. But for Jude, it is not the intellectual remoteness but the social remoteness which strikes him. "Only a wall divided him from those happy young contemporaries of his with whom he shared a common mental life: . . . Only a wall—but what a wall!" That is the note which is struck throughout this section, and when Jude eventually comes to write to the Master of one of the colleges, the reply expresses in its address the reason for rejection, "To Mr. J. Fawley, Stonemason." For the Master, Jude is not there as a person but as a trade, a trade which should not seek to go beyond the walls it is committed to restoring. The social criticism of this section is direct and unequivocal, and the authorial sentiment none the less trenchant for its familiarity: "here in the stone yard was a centre of effort as worthy as that dignified by the name of scholarly study within the noblest of the colleges." But the criticism of Christminster goes beyond a defence of the dignity of labour, it extends to its self-conscious medievalism "as dead as a fern-leaf in a lump of coal." The social astringencies of this section, while they are not remarkable in themselves and, are, indeed, commonplaces in the social writings of critics like Arnold, Ruskin and Morris, nevertheless evoke a very different mood from the first section of the novel with its large metaphysical gestures, its sustained air of cosmic gloom. While this is a mood in which precise social criticisms are emphatically made, nevertheless other notes are being struck in a quiet way which subtilise that criticism. There is a *naïveté* about Jude which is difficult to gainsay. While he might have failed to recognise that "mediaevalism was as dead as a fern-leaf in a lump of coal," he might have made a more effective communication with the colleges if he had chosen a more profitable method of selection than walking the city looking for the heads of colleges and then selecting "five whose physiognomics sccmcd to say to him that they were appreciative and far-seeing men. To these five he addressed letters." This does not blunt the edge of criticism about the attitude of the colleges, but it gives an additional nuance to the epigraph which prefaces the section, "Save his own soul he hath no star." The exclusiveness of that statement is something that Hardy is to look at several times in the course of the novel, but here it is offered in its simplest form. Jude's naïveté, while being related to a fundamental honesty, is also disabling in that it prevents him from taking an adequate measure of the situation in which he finds himself. So that as the section concludes with Jude seeking solace for his rejection in a Christminster pub and being challenged to recite the Nicene Creed to a public for whom it might as well have been "the Ratcatcher's Daughter in double Dutch," our response is not simply that the Christian creed is incomprehensible to "the real life of Christminster," but that Jude himself has a great deal to learn about himself and the world in which he lives.

Is it right to equate education with formal learning? Might an education not be found in a vocation pursued away from the college world of Christminster? It is with questions like these in mind that Jude goes to Melchester to the theological college, with a vague intention to enter the Church, but primarily to be near Sue.

Up to this point Sue's role, lightly sketched in as it has been, would seem clear and unequivocal. She is, among other things, the sceptical voice of the present age, at ease in Christminster, but scornful of its social exclusiveness and even more of its attachment to a creed outworn. The pieties she respects are those of the free spirit; she is wary of the dead hand of the past, sensitive and open to change. For her, Jude is enslaved to a false dream of learning and an idle religious superstition. The kind of conflict which exists between them is succinctly expressed in this exchange:

> "Shall we go and sit in the Cathedral?" he asked, when their meal was finished.
> "Cathedral? Yes. Though I think I'd rather sit in the railway station," she answered, a remnant of vexation still in her voice. "That's the centre of the town life now. The Cathedral has had its day!"
> "How modern you are!"
> "So would you be if you had lived so much in the Middle Ages as I have done these last few years! The Cathedral was

a very good place four or five centuries ago; but it is played
out now."

The unhesitating sharpness of Sue's replies might perhaps alert us to an
authorial irony here, but it is a measure of the feeling of the novel that,
at this stage, it is Jude's reactions which take our attention. With our
reading of the Christminster section behind us, he would still seem to
be the victim of a romantic naïveté, a nostalgic addiction to the past.
And so when sometime later Sue says, "the mediaevalism of Christminster must go, be sloughed off, or Christminster itself will have to
go," we feel that diagnostic confidence evokes sympathy in the author.
When Sue falls foul of the rules governing her training college, we suppose that the kind of criticism against educational institutions operative
in the Christminster sections is simply being extended here—the intellectual rigidities of the one being replaced by the moral rigidities of the
other.

But it is just here, at the centre of the Melchester section, when the
pattern of authorial feeling would seem to be becoming increasingly
defined, that the novel begins to change tack in an extremely interesting
and unexpected way.

Sue having escaped from the confining discipline of the college takes
refuge with Jude, and begins to recall her past: "My life has been entirely
shaped by what people call a peculiarity in me. I have no fear of men,
as such." For the first time we are given a perspective on Sue other than
that of the free spirit, the devoted Hellene, the admiring follower of Mill.
This new impression is developed quickly, so that when she says to Jude,
"You mustn't love me. You are to like me—that's all," we feel a vibra-
tion here which is not that of Sue delicately preserving her commitment
to Phillotson, but rather that of her inability to achieve a commitment
of any kind. The "freedom" she has been at such pains to assert, and
which up to this stage in the novel would seem to have provided an
unequivocal point of vantage for criticising Jude's dream and the institutions which thwart it, is now seen as something much more ambivalent, a nervous self-enclosure, the swift conceptualising, safeguarding
the self against the invasions of experience. Sue's scrutiny is keen, but it
is judiciously angled. The effect of this interplay between her public and
private self emerges in this exchange:

> "At present intellect in Christminster is pushing one way,
> and religion the other; and so they stand stock-still, like two
> rams butting each other."

> "What would Mr. Phillotson—"
> "It is a place full of fetichists and ghost-seers!"
> He noticed that whenever he tried to speak of the school-master she turned the conversation to some generalizations about the offending University.

This is an interesting passage because we can gauge the effect of the personal pressures being exerted on Sue. Her opening remark is of a piece with her general criticism about the intellectual sterility of Christminster and the simile exhibits the familiar self-confidence in her analysis. The effect of Jude's mention of Phillotson is immediately to make that analysis shrill and strained, "it is a place full of fetichists and ghost-seers." Gradually we begin to see that for Sue the pursuit of the idea becomes a surrogate for the presence of personal feeling. The effect of this is not to invalidate the idea, but to make us increasingly aware that, by the end of the Melchester section, the centre of Hardy's interest has moved from the world Jude sees—and with it the criticism provoked by that world—to Sue and "that mystery, her heart."

At the very end of the Melchester section there occurs an incident, insignificant in the general development of the novel, but which expresses in a modest but beautifully precise way the "series of seemings" which the novel as a whole is building up. Greatly moved by a hymn being sung that Easter, "At the Foot of the Cross," Jude feels that the composer is a man who will understand the problems that beset him, and characteristically, resolves to pay him a visit. The meeting is a crushing disappointment—the composer is interested only in his royalties and has turned to the wine trade for greater financial comfort. The ironies are strident and would seem a further variant on the deceptions of appearance, and generally to be taking up the kind of social criticism present in the Christminster section; there is, besides, a gentle deflating of Jude's naïveté. The episode however is to have further implications.

Settled in Shaston—"the ancient British Palladour . . . the city of a dream"—Sue prepares to meet Jude for the first time as Mrs. Phillotson. The afternoon is growing dark and Jude makes his way to the school-room where he expects to find her. Seeing it empty he proceeds to play idly on the piano the opening bars of "At the Foot of the Cross":

> A figure moved behind him, and thinking it was still the girl with the broom Jude took no notice, till the person came close and laid her fingers lightly upon his bass hand. The imposed hand was a little one he seemed to know, and he

turned. "Dont stop," said Sue, "I like it. I learnt it before I left Melchester."

Jude then asks her to play it for him:

> Sue sat down, and her rendering of the piece, though not remarkable, seemed divine as compared with his own. She, like him, was evidently touched—to her own surprise—by the recalled air; and when she had finished, and he moved his hand towards hers, it met his own half-way. Jude grasped it.

It is the renewal of the relationship which is to culminate in Sue's leaving Phillotson and going to live with Jude. The darkening room and the rich melancholy music conspire to weave the spell which enables their relationship to take on an added intensity, an intensity made possible by the fact that the music succeeds in awakening Sue's emotions, but at the same time provides a suitably "spiritual" mode of expression. This episode, coming at the beginning of the Shaston section, initiates an ever-increasing concern with Sue which is to dominate the remainder of the novel.

"We were too free, under the influence of that morbid hymn and the twilight." Sue's self-reproach and resolution to withdraw from Jude's company has a fugitive life, and at Shaston we see the break-up of her marriage with Phillotson and the elopement with Jude. When we look at the series of conversations with Phillotson we can see how far Hardy has now taken us into the area of personal relationships. We can catch it revealingly in this exchange, where Sue is attempting some kind of defence of her marital attitudes to Phillotson:

> "But it is not I altogether that am to blame!"
> "Who is then? Am I?"
> "No—I don't know! The universe, I suppose—things in general, because they are so horrid and cruel!"
> "Well, it is no use talking like that."

That Sue's reference to "the universe" should come over as limply rhetorical—an unfocused irritation—and Phillotson's pragmatism as both just and solicitous, is an index of the change in mood and direction since the opening sections of the novel. Sue's critical intelligence may still be on display, but we feel that she is now very much its victim, in the sense that having announced her wish to leave Phillotson and live with Jude, she quotes Mill by way of justifying her action: "J. S. Mill's words, those are. I have been reading it up. Why can't you act upon them? I wish to, always." If this was not so clearly dictated by emotional desperation, it would simply strike us as callow and grossly insensitive to the situation in which she finds herself. This is enforced by the increasing sympathy with which Phillotson is presented throughout the section. The account of his final evening with Sue is one of the most deeply felt passages in the novel, and all the more so for the restraint and delicate precision of its feeling.

If Jude formally commits himself to Sue now, he does so with an increasing awareness of her enigmatic nature. And Phillotson's generous farewell tones "You are made for each other," echo hollowly in the railway carriage as Sue leaves her husband, only to tell Jude that they are not to be lovers in the way he anticipated. He sees her now in a way that he has not seen her before, and though this does not affect his love, a new sharpness of insight is unquestionably present: "Sue, sometimes, when I am vexed with you, I think you are incapable of real love"; "under the affectation of independent views you are as enslaved to the social code as any woman"; "you spirit, you disembodied creature, you dear, sweet, tantalizing phantom—hardly flesh at all; so that when I put my arms round you I almost expect them to pass through you as through air." And characteristically, Sue's supreme moment of committing herself to Jude is to enter her hotel room—alone.

The deepening analysis of Sue, this is the main preoccupation and drive of this section of the novel, but if we are to understand the remainder of the novel it is important to see that analysis in its context. And it is a context which is increasingly concerned to ponder the meaning of "freedom." All the characters in the Shaston section are, in one way or another, asked to ponder this, Sue, Jude, Phillotson and Gillingham. And this meditation is given sharp emphasis by the incident of the rabbit caught in the gin and mercifully killed by Jude. When Jude comes to reflect on his ruined career at the hands of two women, he uses precisely this imagery: "Is it that the women are to blame; or is it the artificial system of things, under which the normal sex-impulses are turned into devilish domestic gins and springes to hold back those who want to progress?" "The artificial system of things"—it would seem precisely that which Sue, Jude and Phillotson are brought to recognise in Shaston and to be able to set aside. Phillotson gives Sue her "freedom," first to be able to go and live with Jude, and then, if she desires, to marry him. Sue begins a life with Jude and appears to be able to call the terms on which it will be lived. Jude formally turns his back on his ambitions, burning his books, and going to live with the woman he loves. Arabella, by marrying again, removes any obstacle about his re-marriage to Sue. Connections with the past too are formally severed as Aunt Drusilla dies, and with her the old Wessex of legend and "the family curse." In Shaston then, Hardy would appear to wipe the slate clean, to give the characters precisely that freedom of decision they have constantly desired and that definition of self they have longed for. Even in the case of Phillotson, where unhappiness has prompted his action, there is a power of resolution, a revelation of self-knowledge which pre-viously had not been open to him. "The artificial system of things" has now been openly challenged and a fresh significance is given to human decision. It is significant that Aunt Drusilla dies in this section of the novel, because it marks the opposite pole from the doom-laden world of Marygreen; it is the moment when the free and untrammelled self seems triumphant.

This then is the context in which we must see the deepening analysis of Sue—that fine instance of "freedom," the supremely individual case. With her we find displayed the consciousness of self, the innate uncer-tainties, the psychic disturbance with which the fiction of our own day is to make us so familiar. And the end of the Shaston section of *Jude* is the ending of a characteristically modern fiction. The wounded rabbit has been set free from the gin, the artificial system of things has been challenged, the individual will has been triumphantly exercised and, though the past may be painful and the future unknown, the self has been validated.

But for Hardy that picture would be radically incomplete. He does not share the views of a later age. Lawrence voiced the representative twentieth-century criticism when he remarked that Hardy's characters were all cowed by "the mere judgement of man upon them, and when all the while by their own souls they were right." That antithesis would have been alien to Hardy, and the last two sections of *Jude* are there to show that "the mere judgement of man" is for him an inextricable part of man's soul. They enable us to look at "the artificial system of things" from an aspect different from any we have had so far—to draw a dis-tinction between the tragedy of a rabbit and the tragedy of a man. The epigraph to the fifth section establishes the emphasis of the section:

> Thy aerial part, and all the fiery parts which are mingled in thee, though by nature they have an upward tendency, still in obedience to the disposition of the universe they are over-powered here in the compound mass the body.

"The aerial part," "the body," this is the dichotomy to be explored, and with the Phillotson decree made absolute and Arabella marrying again, Sue and Jude are in her words, "just as free now as if we had never married at all." For Jude this has its own significance: "Now we'll strut arm and arm like any other engaged couple. We've a legal right to." But for Sue, such legality is inimical to the freedom she has just painfully re-acquired—it implies a gesture of public commitment which she, and in effect Jude too, are reluctant to make. Her aversion to marriage has nothing to do with uncertainty about her feelings for Jude, but she fears that those feelings will be debased by "the government stamp," by a construct which is no more than "a licence to be loved on the premises." Faced with the idea of a marriage ceremony, she can see only a sequence of external gestures from which all inner significance has been drained. It marks the high points of her self-enclosure—a self-enclosure not disturbed by the widow Edlin's sardonic reminders of a world beyond herself: "Nobody thought o' being afeard o' matrimony in my time, nor of much else but a cannon ball or empty cupboard! Why when I an my poor man were married we thought no more o't than of a game o' dibs!"

Two events however do conspire to modify it. The first is the arrival of Arabella, when feelings of jealousy precipitate Sue into sharing her bed with Jude. The second is more far-reaching—the arrival of Father Time, the natural son of Arabella and Jude, and it is with this figure that Hardy gives his narrative the last decisive shift.

From his introduction Father Time stands apart from the narrative, and of course at the level of realistic presentation he is very awkwardly accommodated indeed. But Hardy leaves us in no doubt that his role is to be choric: "He was Age masquerading as Juvenility, and doing it so badly that his real self showed through the crevices." And as he sits in the railway compartment he "seemed to be doubly awake, like an enslaved and dwarfed Divinity, sitting passive and regarding his companions as if he saw their whole rounded lives rather than their immediate figures." It would be foolish to deny that the attempt to integrate Father Time into the novel is not a success; Hardy has set aside the conventions of realism too easily, so that the child appears to have strayed into the novel from another art form, Lady Macduff's son unnervingly encountered on "The Great Western." But that Hardy should be prepared to risk so much with him is an indication both of the necessity of what he is trying to say at this stage of the novel and of his difficulty in finding a satisfactory way of saying it. In a phrase, he is introducing with Father

Time the processes of history into the lives of Jude and Sue—his sorrowful contemplative eyes become ours as we watch them desperately attempting to cheat time, repudiating the past, evading the social commitments of the present, indifferent, with their ever increasing family, to the demands of the future. With Father Time their "dreamless paradise" fades into the light of common day.

This is poignantly revealed in the visit which Jude and Sue pay to the Great Wessex Agricultural Show. It is one of the rare moments when happiness seems to prevail, and it is also one of the rare moments when we see Jude and Sue through the eyes of others, in this case those of Arabella and Cartlett. The effect is that of a brightly lit picture, darkly framed. Wessex, once a whole way of life, is now present merely as "a show" for itinerant observers. Jude and Sue arrive by excursion and wander through the exhibition ground. Entirely lost in each other's company, they are oblivious of the people around them:

> "Happy?" he murmured.
> She nodded.
> "Why? Because you have come to the great Wessex Agricultural Show—or because *we* have come?"
> "You are always trying to make me confess to all sorts of absurdities. Because I am improving my mind, of course, by seeing all these steam-ploughs, and threshing-machines, and chaff-cutters, and cows, and pigs, and sheep."

What was once a way of life, a history, has now become an inventory for "the improvement" of the mind, and a mind exercised not by things in use, but by things exhibited. Jude, trying to find in the event a crystallisation of his feelings, only moves Sue to a characteristic withdrawal of hers as she marks out, with firm lines of demarcation, the observer from the world observed. If the world observed is to extend her feelings, then it must not be through a shared experience, but through one in which she participates alone.

And so we find her pausing to admire the roses, "I should like to push my face quite into them—the dears!" Like Miriam in *Sons and Lovers,* she can encounter the sensual world only when she can impose herself upon it, when it cannot make reciprocal demands, but is simply there to feed the contemplative soul. Such a moment cannot be sustained, and Father Time reflects that in a few days the flowers will all be withered.

The moment of joy is precarious and the shadows of Arabella and

Father Time, cast emblematically at the Show, begin to acquire a social reality. Ironically, Jude's and Sue's trouble begins with a return to the law which they have both, in their various ways, tried to set aside—a law at once human and divine. Jude, commissioned to re-letter the Ten Commandments in a nearby church, causes a scandal when he is joined in his work by the pregnant, unmarried Sue, and is duly dismissed. His life of wandering now begins, his home is uprooted for the second time, his goods are sold. Father Time asks why they must go, and Jude replies sardonically, "Because of a cloud that has gathered over us; though 'we have wronged no man, corrupted no man, defrauded no man.'" To which Father Time might have added that they have sought to meet no man either. They have neglected "the disposition of the universe," and in consequence the "aerial part" and "the body" have been kept at war.

In Jude's decision to return to Christminster we find a summoning of will and a recognition of the disposition of the universe which has never been present in Sue. For Sue the place still remains what it has always been, "a nest of commonplace schoolmasters whose characteristic is timid obsequiousness to tradition." But for Jude, though he recognises himself as permanently excluded from it, "it is still the centre of the universe. . . . Perhaps it will soon wake up, and be generous." This acceptance of possibilities, of change, is a note which characterises Jude throughout the last tragic section of the novel, a section drawing out a radical difference in response, as Jude and Sue become increasingly enmeshed in the society they have sought to reject.

Once again the epigraph catches the main emphasis, "And she humbled her body greatly, and all the places of her joy she filled with her torn hair." The "aerial part" now seeks to annihilate "the body," and the freedom it seeks is the last freedom of all—the freedom of self-destruction. But "the body" can no longer be thought of as "the individual body," and in destroying herself, Sue destroys the lives of those around her. The full meaning of Father Time is to become clear in this last section where the social body and the individual body become inextricably united, a recall to Hardy's abiding theme that the human race is "one great network or tissue which quivers in every part when one point is shaken, like a spider's web if touched."

Jude's attitude of mind in returning to Christminster is made clear in his speech to the crowd who have gathered for Remembrance Day. Though it is certainly not free from bitterness, it is clear in its emphasis:

It was my poverty and not my will that consented to be

beaten. It takes two or three generations to do what I tried to do in one. . . . Eight or nine years ago when I came here first, I had a neat stock of fixed opinions, but they dropped away one by one; and the further I get the less sure I am . . . I perceive there is something wrong somewhere in our social formulas.

These sentiments give a suggestively defining edge to the way in which Jude has evolved throughout the successive stages of his life—the early metaphysical glooms, the unfocused intellectual and theological ambitions, the formal disavowals and the retreat into self, and now the attempt to come to terms with a social reality which, harsh and forbidding as it might be, is resistant to prophecy and to judgement. As with the Greek and Latin grammars which he received as a boy, there is no simple law of transmutation, there is only a series of seemings. It is this view which Sue is to reject, and the extent of her negation will make plain what is at stake. In the last analysis, by a sad irony, assertions of the free spirit are to catch the inflexible tones if not the substance of Aunt Drusilla's curse.

The narrative now leads into the most terrible scene in Hardy's fiction, indeed it might reasonably be argued in English fiction—the killing of the children by Father Time. Although the scene is brutally disturbing in a way which the novel can hardly accommodate, nevertheless its animating purpose is rooted deep within the evolving structure of the novel, and it does not represent a deflection of Hardy's into a momentary despair, resulting in an episode more akin to *grand guignol* than realistic fiction. The scene is obviously an attempt at the same kind of choric effect as that represented by Father Time himself, a reaching out beyond the particulars of the narrative to an impersonal tragic dimension, a dimension where Time ceases to be a child and becomes "the whole tale of their situation." So that the author can go on to say: "On that little shape had converged all the inauspiciousness and shadow which had darkened the first union of Jude, and all the accidents, mistakes, fears, errors of the last. He was their nodal point, their focus, their expression in a single term." The scene is "the action" of such a figure, the only action he is capable of performing.

To say this is not to argue for the success of the scene, but merely to suggest its nature. It also directs attention to the way in which it arises out of the previous narrative, though its relationship is more with the inner drama than with overt incident. And because it is a drama related to Sue rather than to Jude, it demands a new directness of treatment, now that the two characters are treading rather different paths.

To establish a context for the scene we might go back to a conversation at Shaston, referred to earlier, where Sue asks Phillotson for her freedom. To support her point she quotes Mill:

> "She, or he 'who lets the world, or his own portion of it, choose his plan of life for him, has no need of any other faculty than the ape-like one of imitation.' J. S. Mill's words, those are. I have been reading it up. Why can't you act upon them? I wish to, always."
>
> "What do I care about J. S. Mill!" moaned he.

The ironies cut deep. Hardy, like Sue a warm admirer of Mill, chooses this passage—in which the variety and independence of human behaviour are defended—to expose Sue's rigidities and intolerance of opinions other than her own. And encompassing that is her total inability to enter into Phillotson's feelings; her intellect is at odds with her sensibility. The point is emphasised later when having left Phillotson, she comes to visit him in his illness, though she "did not for a moment, either now or later, suspect what troubles had resulted to him from letting her go; it never once seemed to cross her mind."

It is precisely this mixture of insensibility and forthright statement that she displays again in her conversation with Father Time when they are frustrated in their search for lodgings at Christminster. He begins by asking:

> "Can I do anything?"
>
> "No! All is trouble, adversity and suffering!"
>
> "Father went away to give us children room, didn't he?"
>
> "Partly."
>
> "It would be better to be out o' the world than in it, wouldn't it?"
>
> "It would almost, dear."
>
> "'Tis because of us children, too, isn't it, that you can't get a good lodging?"
>
> "Well—people do object to children sometimes."
>
> "Then if children make so much trouble, why do people have 'em?"
>
> "O—because it is a law of nature."
>
> "But we don't ask to be born?"

"No indeed."

She then goes on to tell the boy that there is to be another baby, but, through a mistaken sense of delicacy, does nothing to remove his impression that she has deliberately sought its arrival. The effect of this on the child—the combination of the indifference of nature's law with the apparent indifference of his mother—is overwhelming. Just as in her previous conversation with Phillotson, Sue is blind to the effect her words will have, and she makes no attempt to go behind the letter of what she is saying. For her, words alone seem certain good.

The situation is now set for the tragedy, and however grotesque the actual incidents that follow, Sue has established a structure of feeling which the boy will carry to a remorseless conclusion, exchanging in his pencilled note of explanation, "Done because we are too menny," literalism for literalism. "The letter killeth" has been made fact. In the icy language of that "explanation," Sue reads her own indictment, and her world is shattered. But imprisoned within extremes, she can only exchange the letter of freedom for the letter of renunciation, and though she recognises that her literalness has provoked the boy's action, she is unable to assimilate the recognition into behaviour, so that she remains unmoved by Jude's agonised response to her proposed remarriage to Phillotson, "Sue, Sue! we are acting by the letter"; and "'the letter killeth!'"

The deaths of the children are a decisive point for her, driving her ever deeper into herself, so that although her behaviour is now in striking contrast to her previous conduct—the return to the church, the remarriage to Phillotson—her fundamental disposition is unchanged. "The aerial part" and "the body" are still held together only by a fanatical act of will, her "enslavement to forms" of self-renunciation replacing her earlier enslavement to forms of self-assertion. Enclosed within herself, she seals herself off almost literally from human communication; "clenching her teeth she uttered no cry" when Phillotson takes her into his bedroom, and when Jude leaves her for the last time she "stopped her ears with her hands till all possible sound of him had passed away." She has transformed herself into pure will.

To turn to Jude is to find that he has continued to move in a significantly different direction. Since his return to Christminster he has increasingly perceived his tragedy to be inextricably involved with time, place and person. "Events did not rhyme as they should," that sentiment stands, but the cause is no longer abstract, metaphysical, nor as Aunt

Drusilla said "sommat in our blood." It is Sue, the free spirit, who now voices that position:

> "All the ancient wrath of the Power above us has been vented upon us, His poor creatures, and we must submit. There is no choice. We must. It is no use fighting against God!"

to which Jude replies:

> "It is only against man and senseless circumstance."

And that remains his attitude to the end. He recognises with perfect clarity his differences from Sue, that "events which had enlarged his own view of life, laws, customs, and dogmas, had not operated in the same manner on Sue's," and more generally: "Strange difference of sex, that time and circumstance, which enlarge the views of most men, narrow the views of women almost invariably." His remarriage with Arabella is a black parody of Sue's with Phillotson, the one made possible only by will, the other through torpor. And it is Jude's remarriage that drives home his own personal tragedy. However much he has come to recognise his tragedy as contingent on circumstance, "the time was not ripe for us! Our ideas were fifty years too soon to be any good to us"; however much he has sought to keep the letter informed by spirit, his own tragedy is stark and unrelieved. Truly, as Hardy says in his preface, Jude's is a tragedy of "unfulfilled aims," and that unfulfilment is both public and private, educational and sexual. It is interesting to notice that in these closing pages Arabella, for all her harshness and cynicism, gives us a sense of being a married woman in a way that Sue never does, and in Jude's refusal to let Sue visit him in his last illness, we feel that finally, he has come to recognise that she could never fulfil that need of his which, however tortuously and casually, is fulfilled by Arabella. His remarriage, of course, can hardly be said to exist at all in its own right, but it is capable nevertheless of casting a harsh restrospective light on Sue, and significantly, the last words of the novel are of Sue's self-deception, and they are spoken not by Jude but by Arabella.

Despite the harsh ironies that attend Jude's death—the cheers from the river sports counter-pointing his recital of verses from the Book of Job, Arabella already preparing herself a future with Vilbert—we feel that Hardy has now opened up perspectives which go beyond the individual tragedy, which reveal the individual as belonging to a wider history, and that it is Jude's singular achievement, despite his personal suffering, to have perceived this.

He never gives up the effort to translate his dream and, even when he returns to Christminster, having seen Sue for the last time, the place is still alive for him with figures of the past. For Arabella, the street is empty, "There's neither living nor dead hereabouts except a damn policeman!" To Arabella, and to Sue in her very different kind of way, Jude's sense of history has no meaning. For the former, the only time is the present, for the latter, time is to be transcended, but for Jude the past is alive in the way that it was for his creator. For them both, things,

> That nobody else's mind calls back,
> Have a savour that scenes in being lack,
> And a presence more than the actual brings.

In that "presence more than the actual" Jude finds, however obscurely, his pledge for the future, and if he comes to reject a Power above us whether beneficent or malevolent, he senses in a recognition of the Spirit of the Years a clue to a proper humanity.

III

I would like to add a last perspective. In July 1914 we find Lawrence writing in a letter to Eddie Marsh:

> Have you got Lascelles Abercrombie's book on Thomas Hardy; and if so, could you lend it me for the space of, say, six weeks; and if so, do you mind if I scribble notes in it? And if you've got any of those little pocket edition Hardy's, will you lend me those, too? . . . I am going to write a little book on Hardy's people.

To come to that "little book" after reading the Wessex novels is to find it a classical postscript. Classical, not in the sense of offering a judicious estimate of the novels—it is too turbulently involved for that—but classical in the sense that it expresses in a remarkably pure way the nature of creative literary influence. Lawrence discerns in Hardy's work elements he feels still inchoate, and through that discernment finds a sharper sense of his own fiction, his own metaphysic. By the end of 1914, "the little book" has become "a sort of Story of My Heart, or a Confessio Fidei." For the modern literary critic it is the workshop for *The Rainbow;* the way in which one kind of fiction becomes transformed into another.

If we read Lawrence's study with a primary interest in Hardy, then it will emerge differently. The critical discussion of Hardy is inset at intervals into Lawrence's own developing argument, and has the function of a series of images in relation to that argument. If we consider the critical discussion apart from its general context, we can see that Lawrence certainly perceived elements and tendencies in Hardy's fiction which remained opaque to the author, but we can also see in that fiction other elements, no less opaque to his critic. By way of illustration we can look at Lawrence's general judgement on the Wessex novels:

> There is a lack of sternness, there is a hesitating betwixt life and public opinion, which diminishes the Wessex novels from the rank of pure tragedy. It is not so much the eternal, immutable laws of being which are transgressed, it is not that vital forces are set in conflict with each other, bringing almost inevitable tragedy—yet not necessarily death, as we see in the most splendid Aeschylus. It is in Wessex, that the individual succumbs to what is in its shallowest, public opinion, in its deepest, the human compact by which we live together, to form a community.

As a description, the criticism corresponds to the case I have tried to argue in [*The Great Web*], but what Lawrence sees as weakness, I have contended is strength. It is precisely the way in which Hardy's fiction moves away from a world where "vital forces are set in conflict with each other," as in *The Return of the Native,* to the world of the later novels where "the human compact" is vividly created, that seems to me to constitute his development as a novelist. Lawrence makes the distinction he has in mind more starkly in a remark I quoted earlier, when he asks about the main characters: "What was there in their position that was necessarily tragic? Necessarily painful it was, but they were not at war with God, only with Society. Yet they were all cowed by the mere judgment of man upon them, and all the while by their own souls they were right." "The mere judgment of man . . . their own souls . . . ," the nerve of the difference in outlook between Hardy and Lawrence lies exposed in that distinction. Hardy's imaginative effort, as his fiction progressed, was directed towards seeing the individual will and the judgement of others in a constant interplay. For Lawrence, that interplay was a friction diminishing the endless variety, the unfinished possibilities that existed within the individual self, and the novel, as "the bright book of life," was there to testify to the reality of those possibilities. If, at the end, for Hardy, in *Jude,* man seems defeated, it is through the obduracy of the world about him, Wessex has faded into the world in which the author wrote.

If we turn again to the way in which *Jude* ends, we can bring Hardy's difficulty into focus, and at the same time see more exactly what is at issue between the novelist who is oppressed by the conflict between the individual soul and the judgement of man, and the novelist who would seek to reject the necessity of a conflict expressed in those terms.

Endings, as I have argued throughout this study, were always a source of difficulty for Hardy, because they implied unity where he sought plurality, they expressed finality where he sought continuity. Hence the variety of strategies he adopted to overcome these constrictions. But *Jude* was to provide him with a particular difficulty because, as I suggested at the beginning of this chapter, the plurality of meaning is expressed in the very form the novel takes, it is an inseparable part of its unfolding movement. There seems nothing within that movement which indicates a natural point of rest, "an ending."

Furthermore, Hardy would seem faced at the end of his novel with making two rather different statements about Jude: he wanted to express the end of his career in terms which are unequivocally and inherently tragic; and also to show that tragedy as contingent on human institutions, on Jude's own failure of temperament. In Lawrence's terms, he wants to combine "the war with God" with the judgement of men. It is the plurality of views carried to its farthest extreme. If, in the final analysis, Hardy fails in his attempt, then I think we should realise that in *Jude* he sought to express an apprehension of contraries so deep that his kind of fiction could no longer accommodate them without collapsing into radical ambiguity or incoherence. But if final success eludes him, his attempt to register this last "series of seemings" is remarkable.

To do justice to the impression of Jude as tragic hero, ravaged and finally destroyed by implacable events, Hardy draws lavishly on the ironies of plot. Jude abandoned by Sue for Phillotson, following the death of the children; Jude tricked and made captive again by Arabella; Jude catching his fatal illness through an abortive visit to Sue in the forlorn hope that she might return to him; Jude dying, alone, reciting the curses of Job, while the university which rejected him is *en fête* outside his windows. It builds up massively into an impression of great poignancy.

For Hardy, however, that impression of the suffering of "the individual soul" has to be offset by another, no less urgent, but much more difficult to convey, the impression of that soul under judgement. It is difficult because it relies on shifting the attitude of the reader to the narrative. And so, running alongside the ironies of plot, Hardy begins to establish what might be described as ironies of tone—ironies calculated to disengage the reader, not from Jude, but from the whole recital of events, so that we can encompass them, rather than become involved in them. The first act of disengagement is Father Time's killing of the children, which, overwhelmingly tragic as it is, is also grotesque, a black parody of certain attitudes of Jude's and Sue's. This sets up within the reader a certain resistance, which enables Hardy to place his central figures in a rather more critical light. Sue's return to Phillotson, however psychologically understandable, is treated in such a way that it borders on the grotesque, and her subsequent life with him serves to confirm that impression. The effect on the reader is that Sue moves away from being a figure of tragedy, into becoming a clinical "case." This, in turn, has its effect on Jude, who for all his increasing alienation from her, still seems helplessly bound to her, so sunk in torpor at her departure that he can even be remarried to Arabella and scarcely notice it. Set against the dead passivity of Sue and Jude, we have the unabated energy of Arabella, plotting with zest and ardour. This builds up into an impression which, pushed further, would not be far removed from the world of black comedy. That is to make the point too strongly, but we can see Hardy at work in these pages not so much redistributing our sympathies, as directing them towards the total situation, and away from the individuals who compose it. One character at least, Arabella, is admirably built to survive into a future beyond the novel, and it is to her that Hardy gives the last words in the book, words free from irony and sharp in their judgement of Sue and Jude: "She's never found peace since she left his arms, and never will again till she's as he is now!" It would be foolish to deny that Hardy intends a harsh irony in the Christminster celebrations which accompany Jude's death and so make us feel the more keenly the desolations of his life. But I think we must also concede that Hardy expresses a sense of the necessary continuity in human living here, and that if Jude finds in the Book of Job a text for cursing, it is also possible to find there a text for endurance. I have no wish to minimise the tragic effect of Jude's death, but I think that there is present at the end of the novel a wider spectrum of feeling than identifying Hardy's "ending" with his death would suggest.

If Hardy does not quite succeed in registering that spectrum with the reader, this is because in *Jude* he has crossed into territory which Lawrence, in particular, was to make peculiarly his own, a territory where the end of the novel points beyond itself and becomes a new beginning. Hardy wrote a fiction which presumed a commission to write about the world as he found it; Lawrence's fiction felt under no such obligation. The novel was the "one bright book of life," its business was "to reveal true and vivid relationships," its commission to make all things new. Whereas it is central to Hardy's purpose to show that Sue's tragedy is, in large measure, due to her failure to come to terms with a history at once public and private, it is central to Lawrence's purpose to reveal Ursula Brangwen's triumph as having behind it precisely that sense of history, but being able to find its climax in vision, which enables her to transcend her past. The generations of history give way to the regeneration of the individual. Such a kind of fiction is bound, by its nature, to be exploratory, with the author no longer content to interrogate the radical contraries *within* his fiction, but seeking always to embody the on-going creative impulse itself, beyond "the end" of his fiction. In such a novel, there is a danger that fictional form will submit to the pressure of authorial testament: it is, at least, a question whether Ursula's vision is supported by the fiction which precedes it. The "end" is less a conclusion, something felt for, expected, within the work itself than a new start, a sense of life awaiting fulfilment. Gerald Crich's remark towards the end of *Women in Love,* "It's a complete experience . . . It's not finished," is Hardy's phrase "a series of seemings" carried to an extreme undreamt of by its author, an extreme where the form of the novel has become *all* process. In *Jude* Hardy was still committed to a fiction which pressed for a conclusion, even though it was to be a conclusion shaken to the core by the pressure of contraries. Looking back, it is difficult to see how that last hard-won ending could have been anything other than the ending to his whole fictional journey. But looking forward, we can see how another novelist was to find a fresh creative impulse in the very difficulties which he saw as characterising that journey: where *Jude* ends *The Rainbow* begins.

The Limits of Art

Terry Eagleton

Jude the Obscure, Hardy's last novel, was first printed as a serial story in *Harper's New Monthly Magazine* from December 1894 to November 1895, and in November 1895 was published as a complete novel. In reply to a warning by Harper's that the novel should "be in every respect suitable for a family magazine," Hardy had doggedly written "that it would be a tale that could not offend the most fastidious maiden"; but Harper's ideal maiden was clearly more fastidious than Hardy's, and the serial version, like *Tess of the D'Urbervilles* before it, had to be heavily bowdlerised. When the novel was finally published as an unexpurgated whole, the critical comment it attracted was mean, bigoted and offensive. A bitter attack in the *New York World* led Hardy to urge Harper's to withdraw the book from circulation; Mrs Oliphant spearheaded the English onslaught with a review in *Blackwood's* entitled "The Anti-Marriage League"; and the Bishop of Wakefield, disgusted with the novel's "insolence and indecency," threw it into the fire. "It is simply one of the most objectionable books that we have ever read in any language whatsoever," commented the *New York Bookman;* and a reviewer in the *World,* betraying the characteristic Victorian middle-class opinion that gloom is somehow socially subversive, remarked that "None but a writer of exceptional talent indeed could have produced so gruesome and gloomy a book."

The effect of all this on Hardy was, in his own words, to cure him completely of further interest in novel-writing. But whether a major

From *Jude the Obscure,* edited by Terry Eagleton. © 1974 by Macmillan Publishers Ltd.

novelist really stops writing simply as a reaction to public opinion is surely doubtful. Hardy was certainly shaken by the mixture of panic, philistinism and hypocrisy his novel evoked, and saw exactly how that response ironically validated the book's case; but there were other reasons for his turning away from fiction. With *Tess of the D'Urbervilles* and *Jude the Obscure*, Hardy had brought his long exploration of the human condition of his society to a point of mature complexity; and, although it would be presumptuous to argue that, after that point, there was nowhere else for him to go, these two novels have a sense of imaginative resolution about them which makes their status as last novels logical rather than fortuitous—something more, anyway, than a submissive bowing to bad reviews. If "resolution" in a different sense wasn't possible—resolution in the sense of providing formulated answers to the conflicts with which these novels deal—this was a mark of Hardy's realism about the limits of art rather than a symptom of despair.

Until quite recently, the story of Jude might have been summarised in a conventional critical account as the tragedy of a peasant boy who uproots himself from a settled and timeless rural community in the pursuit of learning, fails to achieve that worthy ideal through excessive sexual appetite, and in failing reveals the inexorable destiny of man himself, doomed to perpetual unfulfilment on a blighted planet. No part of that statement is in fact true, and to ask why not provides a starting-point for a more accurate reading of the novel. Jude is neither a peasant nor particularly over-sexed; Marygreen, his childhood home, has nothing settled or timeless about it; the Christminster culture which attracts him is shoddy rather than worthy; and his failure to attain it has no "cosmic" significance whatsoever. The novel goes out of its way to emphasise all these facts, and only a reading biased by ideological preconceptions about Hardy's fiction could fail to recognise them.

Jude is not a peasant: that class had long since been destroyed by changes in the social structure of the English countryside. He is the ward of a struggling shopkeeper who has herself declined from socially superior status, becomes a baker's delivery boy and later a stonemason. His place in Marygreen society, in other words, is with the semi-independent "tradesman" class which, as Hardy points out in his essay "The Dorsetshire Labourer" (in *Longman's Magazine*, July 1883), was being decimated by economic depression, increased social mobility and growing industrialisation. As a class, they offered a peculiarly intense focus for the disruptive social forces at work in the countryside, and so are almost always in the centreground of Hardy's fiction; it was the class into which he himself was born, as the son of a stonemason. As part of this class, Jude isn't "uprooted" from Marygreen because there is nothing to be uprooted from. The fact that he doesn't belong to Marygreen in the first place, but was dumped there one dark night (as his own son is later unloaded in Aldbrickham), is significant: Jude's own lack of roots is symptomatic of the generally deracinated condition of the place. Marygreen is not timeless but stagnant, not settled but inert; it is a depressed and ugly enclave by-passed by history, stripped of its thatched and dormered dwelling-houses as the tradesmen, craftsmen and lifeholders move from the land. Like the five bottles of sweets and three buns behind the oxidised panes of Drusilla Fawley's shopwindow, Marygreen is a stale remnant, a plundered landscape denuded of its historical traditions. What has ousted those traditions is utility:

> The fresh harrow-lines seemed to stretch like the channellings in a piece of new corduroy, lending a meanly utilitarian air to the expanse, taking away its gradations, and depriving it of all history beyond that of the few recent months, though to every clod and stone there really attached associations enough and to spare—echoes of songs from ancient harvest-days, of spoken words, and of sturdy deeds.

The abstract imperatives of profit and utility have flattened and levelled all qualitative distinctions and concrete associations in Marygreen, superimposing their directions on the place as rigidly as the harrow-lines do on the fields.

The boy Jude is himself a tool of those imperatives: as the harrow-lines dominate the arable land, so he is compelled for sixpence a day to impose his authority on the birds in the fields by scaring them away with his clacker. Sorry for the birds, Jude rebels against his slavish role and takes a redistribution of resources into his hands: " 'Poor little dears!' said Jude, aloud. 'You *shall* have some dinner—you shall. There is enough for us all. Farmer Troutham can afford to let you have some.' " This view isn't shared by Farmer Troutham, Jude's employer, who assaults him with his own clacker. The punitive, profit-based relations of Marygreen are in clear contradiction with the claims of cultured sensitivity: it is Phillotson, the local representative of "culture," who tells Jude to be kind to animals. Yet, as always in the novel, the relation between ideals and harsh actuality is a dialectical one: the ideal criticises the reality but is in turn exposed by it as limited or utopian. (Thus the novel's original title, "The Simpletons," is both an irony at the expense of the society and a comment on the nature of Jude and Sue's idealism.) Jude's tender gesture prefigures his later courageous affirmations of human solidarity (in the adoption of Father Time, for example), but it is also, of course, amusingly sentimental. When it comes to food, men take priority over birds. Later in the novel Jude is sickened by Arabella's pig-sticking, but her angry comment, "Poor folks must live," has a point, and Jude must learn it.

There is another important sense in which the relation between ideal and reality in the novel is dialectical. The more starved and barren actual life is, the more the ideals it generates will be twisted into bodiless illusions; Jude's "dreams were as gigantic as his surroundings were small." The most obvious instance of this is Christminster. Christminster's phantasmal allure, glimpsed by Jude from the top of his ladder, becomes after his arrival in the city the sinister phantasm of feeling himself spectrally disembodied, stared through by passers-by when he is working (again, with neat irony, on a ladder). If Marygreen is stripped of history, Christminster is buried under it, a repressive rubble of crumbling masonry and dead creeds. The two spots are ominously connected early in the novel, when the man who points out Christminster to Jude gestures in the direction of the field where the boy was beaten by Troutham. Just as Marygreen is swathed in deception and superstition—Vilbert's quack medicine, Arabella's artificial hair, manufactured dimples, false pregnancy and sexual trickery, the sham Gothic edifice which has usurped the traditional church—so Christminster is a maze of false consciousness and sham ceremony which imprisons Jude as effectively as Arabella's wiles. His future turns out, precisely, to be a past; in moving hopefully forward he is rapidly regressing.

The historical irony in which Jude is trapped is that personal fulfilment can be achieved only by painfully appropriating the very culture which denies and rejects him as a man. It is a contradiction in his relation with Christminster which is focused most sharply in the issue of work—a central interest of Hardy's, in this and other novels. As a stonemason trained in the countryside, and so relatively unscathed by an urban division of labour, Jude's work expresses a productive creativity which contrasts strongly with the sterility of the University. He works in direct, responsive relation to the material world; and as such his craft is an image of that attempt to subdue the "insensate and stolid obstructiveness" of things to significant human purpose which is of wider importance in the novel. Craftsmanship, like authentic sexual relationship, mediates between the ideal and the actual. It is in the labour of the

Christminster working class that Hardy discovers an alternative to the decayed world of the dons:

> For a moment there fell on Jude a true illumination; that here in the stone yard was a centre of effort as worthy as that dignified by the name of scholarly study within the noblest of the colleges. . . . He began to see that the town life was a book of humanity infinitely more palpitating, varied, and compendious than the gown life. These struggling men and women before him were the reality of Christminster, though they knew little of Christ or Minster.

In examining the mouldings of the colleges, Jude discovers true historical continuity—not with the elitist University culture, but with "the dead handicraftsmen whose muscles had actually executed those forms," men with whom he feels comradeship. On the basis of this sense of historical continuity, the identity he is seeking could be genuinely established.

Yet the irony, once again, is that Jude's labour-power is exploited literally to prop up the structures which exclude him. His work is restorative of the old world rather than productive of the new, devalued to "copying, patching and imitating." The dead, phantasmal past of Christminster sucks nutriment from the labour of the living, reducing them too to husks and corpses, spectres of their former selves. The true relations between labour and culture, conceived as simple opposites by the deluded Jude of Marygreen, are starkly disclosed in the divided world of Christminster: the cultural ideal is parasitic on working energies it ignores and represses, on labourers without whom "the hard readers could not read nor the high thinkers live."

Sue Bridehead has seen through the cultural ideal, and emancipated herself from the stagnant medievalism of Christminster; but her emancipation is partial and in some ways false. She sees the University as a place "full of fetichists and ghost-seers," but by the end of the novel she herself is both. If Jude can finally extricate himself from false consciousness through the painful process of experiencing the harsh conditions in which such illusions are needed in the first place, Sue's reaction against orthodoxy is idealist: the substitution of one spiritual ideology for another. She is still under the influence of idols: it is merely that statues of Greek deities replace statues of Christian saints on her mantelpiece. If Jude regresses in trying to move forward, so does she: she is "more ancient than medievalism." Jude lives a contradictory relationship with Christminster, strengthening the very walls which exclude him, and finally breaks with ecclesiastical art-work. Sue, the pagan designer of pious texts, lives out a similar conflict, and breaks free to become a teacher; but the deeper contradiction she incarnates is left relatively untouched by this act. Sue is Hardy's most masterly exploration of the limits of liberation in Victorian society—more masterly by far than Angel Clare, who is an earlier experiment in the same mode. As both a chronically timid prisoner of convention and an impetuous rebel, Sue dramatises all the conflicts and evasions of what can best be termed a transitional form of consciousness, deadlocked between the old and the new. The psychological pattern to which that deadlock gives rise is one of masochism and self-torture—a continual process of acting impulsively and then punitively repressing herself for it.

This is most clear in her deep fear of sexuality. *Jude the Obscure* is a novel about passion—passion for human and sexual fulfilment, and its agonised frustration at the hands of a society which must everywhere deny it. Passion is a potentially liberating force in the novel, as Jude shows well enough. With "a simple-minded man's ruling passion," Jude pursues his demand for recognition, refuses to back down from the question of his own identity, and is finally defeated and betrayed. But Jude is a genuinely tragic protagonist because the value released in that defeat, the insistence on a recognition of his total humanity, challenges, consciously or not, a society polarised between abstraction and appetite, labour and intellect. The problem is how to prevent that passion from being tamed and shackled by oppressive convention, and it is this which motivates Sue's rejection of marriage. But her rejection of marriage springs from the same source as her rejection of physical sexuality; in denying the false social embodiments of love, she denies the body itself. Her freedom, as a result, is in part negative and destructive—a self-possessive individualism which sees all permanent commitment as imprisoning, a fear of being possessed which involves a fear of giving. Her scorn for those whose "philosophy only recognises relations based on animal desire" is genuinely progressive in its insistence on fully human relationship and conventionally Victorian in its belittling of physicality. Jude, fresh from the misery of a marriage with Arabella based "on a temporary feeling which had no necessary connection with affinities that alone render a life-long comradeship tolerable," shares Sue's opinion; but, as that "life-long" suggests, he is more inclined to welcome permanent and definitive commitments than she is, and less inclined to see sex as merely incidental to them.

There are other ways in which Jude and Sue differ. It isn't unimportant, for instance, that Sue's individualism springs in part from her reading of J. S. Mill, whose bourgeois notion of the autonomously developing self conflicts with Jude's own more communal and collectivist ethic. His membership of an Artizan's Mutual Improvement Society at Aldbrickham signifies his concern for the advancement of his class as a whole; and that concern for solidarity underlies his decision to adopt Father Time:

> "What does it matter, when you come to think of it, whether a child is yours by blood or not? All the little ones of our time are collectively the children of us adults of the time, and entitled to our general care. That excessive regard of parents for their own children, and their dislike of other people's, is, like class-feeling, patriotism, save-your-own-soul-ism, and other virtues, a mean exclusiveness at bottom."

Sue agrees that "if [Father Time] isn't yours it makes it all the better," but for rather less altruistic reasons: she is reluctant to have his child by a previous marriage in the house. It is a difference between them which emerges again at the end of the book: Jude behaves "honourably" towards Arabella because he is not "a man who wants to save himself at the expense of the weaker among us," whereas Sue, in her guilty return to Phillotson, is in the end such a woman. Even Jude can see this—can see that Sue has degenerated to a save-your-souler. "I stuck to her, and she ought to have stuck to me. I'd have sold my soul for her sake, but she wouldn't risk hers a jot for me."

But this is to be too hard on Sue and not hard enough on Jude. Sue does, after all, give herself fully to Jude for a brief period of happiness, and the events which drive her back to Phillotson are horrific enough to make her betrayal understandable, if not excusable. And, if Sue is elusively unpossessable, Jude for his part is too ready to be appropriated, too uncritically willing to be the adopted son of the deathly lineage of Christminster. If Sue is finally enslaved by ghosts and fantasies, Jude has been so all along. It is a choice between that genuine disentanglement from delusion at which Jude must laboriously arrive, by which time his energies are spent, and the more rapid emancipation of Sue which, because it is ungrounded from the outset in much more than a mental conversion, is unable to withstand the buffetings of reality.

What is remarkable, in fact, is how Hardy retains some of our sympathy for Sue against all the odds. For there isn't, when one comes down to it, much to be said in her defence. Having speeded on the death of her first lover, Sue captivates Jude to enjoy the thrill of being loved, and then enters with dubious motives and curiously mechanical detachment into marriage with Phillotson, treating Jude with astounding callousness in the process. Having refused to sleep with Phillotson she abandons him for Jude, temporarily wrecking the schoolmaster's career, and refuses to sleep with Jude too. She then agrees to marry him out of jealousy of Arabella, changes her mind, and finally returns again to Phillotson, leaving Jude to die. It's clear that such an external account of Sue's behaviour is inadequate as a basis for total judgement, but it's also important not to slide too quickly over the incriminating facts. The problem is how we come to feel that Sue *is* more than just a perverse hussy, full of petty stratagems and provocative pouts; for that this is at one level an accurate description of her seems undeniable. One reason why we feel that she is more than this is, of course, because she is so deeply loved by Jude; but Jude's love of Sue, like his love of Christminster, is an authentic desire refracted through a flawed medium, and he himself comes at times as near as possible to seeing her in a much less attractive light. The answer to the enigma of Sue seems to lie, not in balancing her undoubtedly "good" qualities against her more unpleasant characteristics, but in reconsidering the question of the "level" at which Sue is finally to be evaluated. After Jude has complained that Sue wouldn't risk her soul for him, he adds that it wasn't her fault; and it is important to see here that Jude is both wrong (he is sentimentally idealising her, as he did before he had even met her), and in a different sense right. It isn't Sue's fault, not because she is morally innocent, but because Hardy, through his presentation of Sue, is evoking movements and forces which can't be exhaustively described or evaluated at a simply personal level. Sue, like Jude himself, is a "representative" character, in the great tradition of nineteenth-century realism which Hardy inherited; and her elusive complexity stems in part from the fact that she points beyond herself, to a confused, ambiguous structure of feeling which belongs to the period in general. Her opaqueness and inconsistency as a character are thus neither merely personal attributes nor evidence of some failure of full realisation on Hardy's part; it is precisely in her opaqueness and inconsistency that she is at once most fully realised and most completely representative. If she were a "fully rounded" character, as wholly knowable as, say, Eustacia Vye in *The Return of the Native,* it would be easier to treat her as an autonomous moral agent, meriting directly personal praise or blame; but she would be also to that extent narrowed, simplified, unrepresentative.

Hardy described the novel in his preface as dramatising "a deadly war waged between flesh and spirit," and it seems worth trying to unpack some of the meanings of that phrase. It is tempting to think of it first of all in terms of a conflict between Arabella and Sue—or rather of those aspects of Jude which each woman is supposed to externalise. But to reduce the novel to an interior battle between appetite and ideal is surely to over-simplify. It isn't just that Sue can only in a very qualified sense be taken as some "ideal"; it's also that Arabella is an equally unobvious candidate to fulfil the role of "appetite." The soft smack of the pig's pizzle which Arabella throws at Jude signifies, evidently enough, a materialist deflation of his priggish dreams of grandeur; but Arabella herself is far from symbolising the lure of some earthy sensuality which impedes Jude's striving for spiritual development. This is true at the level of plot—it isn't Arabella who prevents Jude from entering the University—and true also of the way she is characterised. What we remember about Arabella isn't her sensuality but her calculating acquisitiveness, her sharp, devious opportunism. She uses her sensual appeal twice to captivate Jude, but what she captivates him for is, in the end, economic security. Arabella is one of a financially insecure class who need to look sharp in a predatory society: "Poor folks must live" is her watchword from beginning to end. The claim on Jude which she represents is less that of some symbolic abstraction like "sensuality" or "appetite" than the need for material provision in conditions of scarcity; she wants to utilise his labour to buy herself frocks and hats, as Christminster uses it to sustain its elaborate façades.

Whereas Jude and Sue struggle bravely against empty convention, Arabella recognises the artifice of those conventions but manipulates them pragmatically for her own advantage. "Life with a man is more business-like after [marriage]," she tells Sue, "and money matters work better." Fly and practical as she is in contrast with Sue, her investment in conventions which she basically scorns offers a parallel to Sue's position, and indeed the two women are alike in more than this. Both are individualists, and both exploit Jude: Arabella crudely and materially, Sue subtly and spiritually. (It is interesting that Jude's entry into relationship with Arabella is characterised less by the prodding of "appetite" than by a sense of dreaming and drifting which resembles his first feelings about Sue.) Arabella, indeed, recognises the similarities between herself and Sue ("Bolted from your first, didn't you, like me?"), a parallel which Sue snobbishly refuses. In terms of the comparison, Arabella comes off in some ways rather better: there's a crude but candid authenticity about her desire for Jude ("I must have him. I can't do without him. He's the sort of man I long for") which contrasts tellingly with the evasions of a woman who, as Jude complains, can never say directly whether she loves him or not. Arabella is able to throw over her false religious conversion and fatalistically acknowledge the thrust of her real feelings for Jude ("Feelings are feelings!"); Sue moves in precisely the opposite direction, disowning her true feelings for Jude for a fatalistic adherence to religious orthodoxy.

Sue's action in abandoning Jude for Phillotson is, in a precise, Sartrean sense of the term, one of bad faith. The attempt to live authentically in a false society collapses into guilty self-punishment, a flight from freedom into the consoling embrace of an impersonal system of authority which will relieve one of the burden of selfhood, and so of responsibility. Sue, the celebrator of a pagan joy in life, becomes the woman who is glad her children are dead, eager to flay her flesh and bring her body into corpse-like submission to a man she physically detests. There is no need for this society to crush those who make the break for freedom; the roots of its deathly ideology sink sufficiently deep in the mind for the self to act as its own censor, anxiously desiring its own extinction.

Jude fights hard against Sue's death-dealing fantasy. "It is only [a fight] against man and senseless circumstance," he argues, in response to her demands for conformity to "the ancient wrath of the Power above us." His argument merely rehearses Sue's own earlier opinion that the roots of the tragedy are social—that "the social moulds civilization fits us into have no more relation to our actual shapes than the conventional shapes of the constellations have to the real star-patterns." The deadly war between flesh and spirit is fundamentally a war between the spirit of man and the obstructive flesh of a recalcitrant society. Sue's attempt to absolutise a particular tragedy as an act of Providence is the most dangerous form of false consciousness, relieving of responsibility the true killer of her children—the society which turned the family from its lodging-houses. It is a mark of Jude's resilience and rationality that he refuses to make this error: absolute as the tragedy is for him, he sees it nonetheless as historically relative. "When people of a later age look back upon the barbarous customs and superstitions of the times that we have the unhappiness to live in, what *will* they say!" He reflects that "It takes two or three generations to do what I tried to do in one," and is interested to hear of schemes already afoot to help poor scholars into Christminster.

Two elements in the novel might seem to argue for Sue's fatalism. One is the emphasis on a hereditary curse in the Fawley family; the other is the role of Jude's son, Father Time. The factor of heredity certainly crops up from time to time, but in the end little is made of it, and it isn't an element in the final tragic catastrophe. It remains as an awkwardly unintegrated dimension of the novel, generating "atmosphere" but not much else; and even if it is taken seriously it seems to amount to no more than Mrs Edlin's judgement that there is a temperamental instability in the family which unfits them for coping with difficulties ("But things happened to thwart 'em, and if everything wasn't vitty they were upset"). Then there is Father Time, who for so many critics has stood for an authentic authorial consciousness, gloomy, pessimistic and omniscient. But it isn't only that Father Time, for all the ponderous symbolism which surrounds him, has essentially the limited understanding of a child, killing himself and the other children on the basis of what is really a mistake—a breakdown of communication between himself and an adult. It's also that Father Time's pessimism springs from the weary passivity of a character who is outside history, unable to intervene constructively in it, condemned (like the naturalistic novelists of the period) to see things in a rounded, distanced, deterministic way. This is not, in fact, Hardy's way: Father Time is rather like the God in Hardy's poems who, precisely because of his transcendental, unhistorical status, is doomed to impotence and disillusion. Father Time can assume his omniscient, spectatorial stance only because his living will has been effectively destroyed; and in this he differs from his father, whose will does not consent to be beaten, and who continues to struggle almost until the end. *Jude the Obscure,* like all of Hardy's novels, proclaims no inexorable determinism, though anyone aware of the paltry percentage of working-class undergraduates now at Oxford might be forgiven for thinking differently.

Vision and Blindness

Norman Page

The metaphorical function of vision and blindness, modes of seeing and failing to see, interpretation and misinterpretation of the visible, is nowhere more evident than in *Jude the Obscure*. When Hardy wants to show a character drawing nourishment from an illusion, he habitually shows him as seeing incompletely or imperfectly, as Jude over and again sees an ideal and not a real Christminster. For an example of the opposite—the sudden perception of a truth conveyed in terms of a clearing of vision—we can turn to *Far from the Madding Crowd:* when Bathsheba announces that Boldwood has shot Troy, the announcement has "somewhat the effect of setting the distorted images in each mind present into proper focus." The observers and non-participants who are such familiar Hardyan character-types, as they contemplate life from the periphery of the sphere of action, are enabled to see with unusual clarity; but if detachment brings discovery and revelation, involvement can entail a loss of vision.

The early pages of *Jude the Obscure* recall Dickens's account in *Great Expectations* of his hero's gaining his "first most vivid and broad impression of the identity of things." As a child, Jude is exceptionally sensitive to his surroundings, and unusually observant of small things as well as large: the opening chapter shows him looking down a well, as if straining to see what the future holds, and soon he is walking carefully down a damp path to avoid crushing the earthworms that most boys would not even have noticed. In the third chapter, he climbs to the roof of a barn

From *Thomas Hardy.* © 1977 by Norman Page. Routledge & Kegan Paul, 1977.

under repair and from that vantage-point strains his eyes (the expression is Hardy's and is used twice in this passage) to see the distant city of Christminster. A friendly workman tells him

> "Christminster is out across there, by that clump. You can see it—at least you can on a clear day. Ah, no, you can't now."
>
> The other tiler . . . had also turned to look towards the quarter designated. "You can't often see it in weather like this," he said. "The time I've noticed it is when the sun is going down in a blaze of flame, and it looks like—I don't know what."
>
> "The heavenly Jerusalem," suggested the serious urchin.

Christminster is there, but invisible; it is a real city, but also, to Jude, a city of the mind and spirit; he knows its geographical location, but simultaneously it belongs to the same order of existence as the heavenly city of "the Apocalyptic writer" (in the New Testament, the Epistle of Jude is immediately followed by the Revelation). Later in the evening he returns, reascends the ladder, and again scans the horizon; this time he sees, or seems to see, Christminster, but the experience is curiously equivocal:

> It was Christminster, unquestionably; either directly seen, or miraged in the peculiar atmosphere.
>
> The spectator gazed on and on.

The force of that "unquestionably" seems weakened by the unusual epithet "miraged," itself a somewhat ambiguous term. A mirage may be an optical illusion produced by certain atmospheric conditions and explicable in scientific terms, while in emotional terms acting as a source of false hopes and subsequent disappointment—and of such a nature Jude's experience of Christminster turns out to be; or it can be, in the words of the *OED,* "the appearance in the sky of a reflected image of a distant object," permitting a visual experience different from the customary one afforded by an object or scene substantial enough in itself. The reader is thus prepared for the paradoxical role of Christminster, as both an actual city and the city of Jude's dreams. Indeed, in the passage under discussion, "dreams" is a significant and recurring word; already the sharpness of the hero's perception of reality is blunted, and he has now begun to see things through a glass darkly. (An interesting parallel is offered in the same passage by the "old woman's 'shop' window, with its twenty-four little panes set in lead-work, the glass of some of them oxidized with age, so that you could hardly see the poor penny articles exhibited within.")

The spectacle, or vision, of the "far-off city" is the first of three views of Christminster sought by Jude as, over a period of years, he draws steadily nearer to his goal of reaching the city; and the three incidents form a progressive pattern in the novel that can hardly be accidental. The first of them is the boyish experience already referred to. The first part of the story, following Hardy's own division, ends with Jude perceiving "the faint halo, a small dim nebulousness, hardly recognizable save by the eye of faith," and resolving to set off for Christminster: again the language of Hardy's prose, with the associations of *halo,* spiritual as well as pictorial, thrown into question by the reiteration of "faint . . . dim . . . ," and the characteristic phrase "the *eye* of faith" is worth close attention. At the beginning of the second part, with marriage to Arabella and separation from her behind him, Jude is found walking towards the city "at a point a mile or two to the southwest of it," and from there he obtains "his first near view of the city." Seen from this second and much closer vantage-point it no longer has the remote and magical quality of the earlier vision, though the time of day is the same and the rays of the setting sun are still reflected by the buildings of the medieval city, which "now lay quiet in the sunset, a vane here and there on their many spires and domes giving sparkle to a picture of sober secondary and tertiary hues." However, once within the city, Jude's perceptions are seen to be modified and distorted by his preconceptions: setting out after nightfall and wandering in its "dark corners which no lamplight reached," he sees only those aspects of the city which appear to harmonize with the Christminster of his dreams: "When he passed objects out of harmony with its general expression he allowed his eyes to slip over them as if he did not see them." Again, the obscurity, like the "rottenness of the stones" of the ancient buildings, is symbolic as well as realistic and pictorial; and the vocabulary of seeing is persistent. Jude's absorption in a world of his own imagining—almost as remote from the real Christminster as from the earthy *milieu* of Arabella—is made plain to the reader by his sense of isolation, of being what Hardy calls "a self-spectre," "almost his own ghost," experiencing the sensation "of one who walked but could not make himself seen or heard." (The theme recurs in the poem "Wessex Heights," written shortly afterwards.)

Jude's third view of Oxford, somewhat later, is obtained from within its heart—more precisely, from the lantern of the Sheldonian

Theatre. It represents a turning-point in his mental life and the onset of disillusion: the time is characterized as "the afternoon on which he awoke from his dream," and the panoramic view afforded by the Sheldonian provides a vision of reality, as the dark corners of the city glimpsed at night had nurtured his groundless ambitions: "it had windows all round, from which an outlook over the whole town and its edifices could be gained." As often, a clear view of physical objects is accompanied by mental or emotional insights—in this case, that "those buildings . . . were not for him." The experience is quickly reinforced by the curt letter from the head of a college, advising him to abandon his notions of a scholar's career and to stick to his trade.

These three views of Christminster thus trace the graph of Jude's hopes and disappointments in the early part of the novel. After the third, he still believes that Christminster is worth attaining, though compelled to accept that it is not for such as he. What Hardy seems to have presented in this earlier portion of his novel is a pattern of three related stages of experience: Jude's initial clear-sightedness is followed by blindness or blinkered vision under the temporary but powerful influence of an outside agency, the loss of sight being itself followed by an eventual realization of the truth and a regaining of accurate perceptions, or at least perceptions which have shed some of the grosser elements of self-deception. Of this kind is Jude's changing consciousness of Christminster in relation to his own life. His idealistic notion of what the city stands for produces a temporary blindness to the reality around him in the intensity of his attention to the inward vision: the observant boy of the opening chapters becomes the youth who hardly notices the "peeps of country" as he walks along, preoccupied as he is by his dreams of Christminster. At another such moment of abstraction from his material surroundings, however, reality asserts itself abruptly and shockingly:

> In his deep concentration on these transactions of the future Jude's walk had slackened, and he was now standing quite still, looking at the ground as though the future were thrown thereon by a magic lantern. On a sudden something smacked him sharply in the ear, and he became aware that a soft cold substance had been flung at him, and had fallen at his feet. A glance told him what it was.
>
> (chap. 6)

The transition from an inward "looking" at what does not exist to the actual seeing of a physical object thrust into the foreground of his attention is significant. The pig's pizzle thrown by Arabella—one of Hardy's most effective symbols, both bold and apt—shatters his contemplative mood as Arabella herself is to shatter the "future" which Jude is envisaging; and under the spell of her sexual attractiveness he undergoes a second and parallel experience of the vision-blindness-vision pattern already described. At first he sees clearly enough: "A glance told him" what the unconventional missile was, and the description of the scene observed by Jude from the other side of the fence (the small homestead and the country girls washing the pigs' chitterlings in the running water) is vividly realistic. But the Circe-like power of Arabella operates quickly, and his clear vision, after a final brief moment of illumination, is lost:

> It had been no vestal who chose *that* missile for opening her attack on him. He saw this with his intellectual eye, just for a short fleeting while, as by the light of a falling lamp one might momentarily see an inscription on a wall before being enshrouded in darkness.

By way of partial (though unsatisfactory) compensation for this loss of vision, his love for Arabella casts its own peculiar light upon the real world and modifies the appearances of objects thereby. When Jude revisits the spot where they have kissed for the first time, he sees the scene not in its objective reality but coloured by his infatuation ("a pollard willow stood close to the place, and that willow was different from all other willows in the world"); and when, in her company, he climbs a summit from which the region around Christminster can be seen, he is blind to the existence of the city for a glimpse of which he has formerly strained his eyes. Hence the repeated references to Samson (Jude twice sees a picture of Samson and Delilah): for Jude too, love is a folly leading to blindness.

Seeing, then, in its various literal and metaphoric forms and in its absence, pervades the novel at the levels of both narrative and style. For Jude it is an activity executed with varying degrees of success at different stages in his history. But he is, as well as being an observer, a doer and a maker; and Jude Fawley's commitment, in the earlier part of the novel, to ecclesiastical architecture and to the Gothic and Neo-Gothic styles is intimately related to some of its major themes. He comes to Christminster at a moment when the extensive repair and restoration of medieval buildings is in progress: specifically, "the Cathedral repairs" involve the overhauling of "the whole interior stonework . . . , to be largely replaced by new." In the stoneyard where he seeks employment, he observes the contrast between old and new in masonry:

> He asked for the foreman, and looked round among the new traceries, mullions, transoms, shafts, pinnacles, and battlements standing on the bankers half worked, or waiting to be removed. They were marked by precision, mathematical straightness, smoothness, exactitude: there in the old walls were the broken lines of the original idea; jagged curves, disdain of precision, irregularity, disarray.

In such passages symbolic meanings seem to be thrusting rather vigorously through the literal statements. In the language of the previous paragraph, the new stone represents "ideas in modern prose"—nineteenth-century rationalism—in contrast to the "old poetry" of the college buildings, survivors of an age of mental obfuscation. The whole passage is, however, somewhat puzzling. Hardy's attitude to Gothic seems ambiguous at this point: Gothic charm is dismissed as an accidental by-product of time (the "lichened colleges . . . had done nothing but wait, and had become poetical"); moreover, the symbolism of the paragraph quoted above is weakened by the fact that the purpose of modern restoration is to replace the "original idea" of ancient architectural features, not to improve on it. His attitude to Neo-Gothic is, however, quite unambiguous, as the following comment makes clear:

> [Jude] did not at that time see that mediævalism was as dead as a fern-leaf in a lump of coal; that other developments were shaping in the world around him, in which Gothic architecture and its associations had no place.

The embodiment of those "other developments" is Sue Bridehead; and the notion of the irrelevance of medievalism—in the teaching of Christminster and its habits of thought and belief no less than in the physical fabric of its buildings—is central in the development of Jude's relationship with Sue, in which the instinctive championing of contrasting artistic styles is a symptom of a basic difference of temperaments. When Jude proposes a visit to Wardour Castle, she objects that it is "'Gothic ruins—and I hate Gothic!'"; and later she tells Jude that he should "'have learnt Classic. Gothic is barbaric art, after all. Pugin was wrong, and Wren was right.'" Unconsciously Sue arouses Greek rather than Christian associations by her appearance: at various times she is compared to "the figures in the Parthenon frieze" and "a Ganymedes"; and in one of those improbable but not impossible episodes characteristic of Hardy's instinct for finding a precise visual counterpart to an abstract idea, on a solitary walk she comes across a group of plaster statuettes, "reduced copies of ancient marbles," placed on the grass "almost in a line between herself and the church towers" of Christminster. While Sue rejects Gothic and all it stands for, Jude retains a love of medieval architecture as exemplified by Christminster even when his disillusion with the city as a satisfactory intellectual and spiritual home is complete. Even when he is unable to work at his craft, he expresses his commitment to the city of his dreams and visions by making "Christminster cakes." As Sue explains to Arabella:

> "They are reminiscences of the Christminster Colleges. Traceried windows, and cloisters, you see. It was a whim of his to do them in pastry."
> "Still harping on Christminster—even in his cakes!" laughed Arabella. "Just like Jude. A ruling passion."

But by this time the attachment is sentimental and nostalgic rather than deriving from a deep conviction of the reality of Christminster values.

Jude, then, is one for whom the visible world powerfully exists, one endowed by nature with an exceptional capacity "to notice such things," as Hardy wrote of himself in a much-anthologized poem ("Afterwards"). His vision is, however, obscured by two separate causes which appear to be working in opposition to each other, but which unite in inducing a disastrous blindness to truth and reality. One is the power of the sex-urge, represented by the Delilah-like Arabella; the other his youthful dreams of Christminster as an earthly Jerusalem. He is a worker in stone, a maker of churches and houses; yet he also builds castles in the air (his old great-aunt observes that, as a child, he had a trick "of seeming to see things in the air"), and his yearning to forsake substantial buildings for ethereal ones is at the root of his misfortunes. The bitterness of his defeat resides in his belated recognition that Christminster is a sham, less a home of godliness and good learning than a bulwark of complacent archaism and irrelevance: it is as unworthy of his longings and his efforts as Sue is (as he tells her in his agony the last time he sees her) "not worth a man's love."

Jude, like most of Hardy's other novels, was illustrated on its first appearance before the public; but the illustrations were in a sense superfluous, for Hardy—whose "quizzical bright eyes" Virginia Woolf noted even near the end of his life—has provided his own "pictures" within the text, and indeed conducts the business of story-telling, here and elsewhere, largely by their means. That the pictorial element is so much more evident in the major than in the minor novels may well be an index of the extent to which the former embody a much fuller involvement of Hardy's imaginative (image-making) powers.

Sue Bridehead, "The Woman of the Feminist Movement"

Kathleen Blake

> *Curiously enough, I am more interested in the Sue story than in any I have written.*
> *Sue is a type of woman which has always had an attraction for me, but the difficulty of drawing the type has kept me from attempting it till now.*
> HARDY to Florence Henniker, August 12, 1895

Hardy's fascination with Sue Bridehead has been shared by many readers, some of whom feel she takes over *Jude the Obscure* from Jude. She is complex to the point of being irresistible, mystifying, or for some exasperating. She seems to Yelverton Tyrell, writing in 1896, "an incurably morbid organism" and to Desmond Hawkins, more than half a century later, "just about the nastiest little bitch in English literature."

Sue Bridehead will be more fascinating than frustrating to those who can find a thread that makes her windings worth following, and who can recognize in her mazes something more than the uniqueness of neurosis. Tyrell asks, "Why dwell on this fantastic greensickness?" Albert Guerard answers for the "minute responsibility" of Hardy's characterization, and Michael Steig argues her psychological coherence in clinical terms. Havelock Ellis and Robert Heilman carry the argument for our interest beyond the psychological consistency of what looks odd in Sue, to its representative importance.

Clearly Hardy thought Sue represented a type, however brilliantly individualized. She herself says that she is not such an exception among women as Jude thinks, particularly on the subject of marriage. She also

From *Studies in English Literature 1500–1900* 18, no. 4 (Autumn 1978). © 1978 by William Marsh Rice University.

says that she and Jude are not alone in their peculiarities. An important passage in Hardy's postscript of 1912 to the preface of *Jude* pinpoints Sue's type as "the woman of the feminist movement—the slight, pale 'bachelor girl'—the intellectualized, emancipated bundle of nerves that modern conditions are producing." By including it in his postscript, Hardy seconds the opinion of a German critic who wrote to him on Sue's feminism. No one seems to know who this German critic was. In fact the passage has been pretty much ignored. Some contemporary reviewers, such as Tyrell, classed *Jude* with "the fiction of Sex and the New Woman." And Hardy seems to have seen the novel in similar terms. When he contemplated dramatizing it, his projected titles were "the New Woman" or "A Woman with Ideas." But this view of the novel fell rather quickly from sight. Only recently has it begun to reappear, as in Lloyd Fernando's *"New Women" in the Late Victorian Novel* and A. O. J. Cockshut's *Man and Woman, A Study of Love in the Novel.* An essay by Mary Jacobus recognizes the conflict between Sue's desire to be an individual and the "femaleness that breaks her" but sets the struggle in rather narrowly personal terms so that her feminism remains disconnected from a wider Victorian framework. A similar lack of contemporary ideological framework causes Kate Millett [in *Sexual Politics*] to doubt Sue's coherence as a character because in her the new woman is at odds with the "frigid woman." I think that to place Sue in relation to Victorian thought on the woman question is to reveal the coherence of this "woman of the feminist movement," whose daring and precise logic of emancipation also produces its rending tensions. The feminism by which Sue frees her brilliant individuality makes her a "frigid woman" at the same time that it keeps her in constant peril of the "femaleness that breaks her."

Most criticism may have steered clear of feminist analysis of the novel because it is widely agreed that Hardy was doctrinaire in no cause or philosophy. He himself disclaims in a letter to Edmund Gosse that *Jude* is simply a problem novel on the marriage question. While not an avowed feminist, he knew something about feminist ideas. For instance, he quotes Tennyson's *Princess* in *The Mayor of Casterbridge* (1886). His library contained such examples of late-century new-woman fiction as Olive Schreiner's *Story of an African Farm,* Sarah Grand's *The Heavenly Twins,* and Grant Allen's *The Woman Who Did.* He sympathized with certain feminist views. If the divorce issue is not all there is to *Jude*, it is part. Hardy also knew and cared about certain women who were touched by the cause.

His first wife Emma was interested in women's rights, but the two models usually proposed for Sue Bridehead are Tryphena Sparks and Florence Henniker. While Robert Gittings's biography of Hardy shows that Tryphena Sparks must have been at least what Victorians called a "strong-minded woman," Florence Henniker was the more demonstrably an "enfranchised woman." Hardy's letters characterize her in these terms. One letter indicates that he plans to get the *Subjection of Women*. This directly implies Mrs. Henniker's feminist interests and their influence on Hardy. However, she was apparently not cut to any stock pattern. Hardy says that he is surprised at her agreeing with Mill. This response is difficult to interpret. But it seems of a piece with his disappointment that a woman in some senses "enfranchised" should be in others conventional, for instance in her religious beliefs. A woman emerges contradictory in her views—like Sue—with the contradictions of a new type. Florence Henniker herself wrote fiction, and one of her heroines called forth Hardy's admiration—"the girl . . . is very distinct—the modern intelligent mentally emancipated young woman of cities, for whom the married life you kindly provide for her would ultimately prove no great charm—by far the most interesting type of femininity the world provides for man's eyes at the present day." This sounds like Sue's type. The heroine's mistake, the conventional marriage, reflects what for Hardy was the similarly mistaken conventionality sometimes shown by her creator and, presumably, prototype.

Lloyd Fernando contrasts *Jude* to other new-woman fiction of the period whose heroines' perfection is made out of theories, not psychological probability. Hardy shows how and why Sue Bridehead is a free woman but a repressive personality, sophisticated but infantile, passionate but sexless, independent but needing men, unconventional but conventional, a feminist but a flirt. He observes her with such undogmatic exactness, with such pure fascinated tenacity, that he shows us how this "bundle of nerves" works, and how her nerves go wrong.

Sue Bridehead wants to free herself of the worst of a woman's fate. Hardy outlines that fate in the section on the young women at the Melchester Training School:

> they all lay in their cubicles, their tender feminine faces upturned to the flaring gas-jets . . . every face bearing the legend "The Weaker" upon it, as the penalty of the sex wherein they were moulded, which by no possible exertion of their willing hearts and abilities could be made strong while the inexorable laws of nature remain what they are.

Hardy gives two versions of the reason for women's hard lot. One is social. When Sue compares a bride to a sacrificial heifer, Jude answers that women should not protest against the man but against the conditions that make him press her. But the narrator charges masculine nature itself when he says that Sue is ignorant of "that side of [men's] natures which wore out women's hearts and lives." Hardy is able to have his sexual disaster both ways by piling one on top of the other. When Sue says "it is none of the natural tragedies of love that's love's usual tragedy in civilized life, but a tragedy artificially manufactured," he implies that, even take away the artificial, the natural tragedy would still remain.

The tragedy begins with sex. Hardy describes the students in the Melchester School with tender nostalgia: their hurry to shed the temporary immunity from the "deadly war" of passion provided by their "species of nunnery" only gives them longer to regret its loss. The young women are preoccupied with last year's seduction, young men who may turn out not to be cousins, late hours, and interesting delinquencies. They are safe, but restless, in the blockaded sexuality of their college regimen:

> They formed a pretty, suggestive, pathetic sight, of whose pathos and beauty they were themselves unconscious, and would not discover till, amid the storms and strains of after-years, with their injustice, loneliness, child-bearing, and bereavement, their minds would revert to this experience as to something which had been allowed to slip past them insufficiently regarded.

Hardy's position is clear. Women suffer by the operations of sexuality—injustice, loneliness, child-bearing, and bereavement. Children bring suffering, Mrs. Yeobright says to little Johnny Nunsuch in *The Return of the Native* (1878). Mother woe is one's personal suffering and the knowledge of having given birth only to suffering. *The Well-Beloved* (1897), written just before *Jude,* expresses another liability of motherhood, that it stunts as well as afflicts. Mrs. Pine-Avon illustrates the rule that the "advance as girls [is] lost in their recession as matrons." Why? "Perhaps not by reason of their faults as individuals, but of their misfortune as child-rearers." By the same token marriage offers no great advantage to a woman. Hardy thinks it is wrong for Florence Henniker's advanced young heroine to marry. There is an interesting late letter recounting the news of his sister-in-law's successful confinement. He responds to the glad tidings with an opposite sentiment: "if I were a woman I should think twice before entering into matrimony in these days of emancipation when everything is open to the sex."

The Training-School students enjoy temporary immunity from sexual disaster. Enforced from without, it is, with all of its repressiveness, yet a haven to be missed later. Sue Bridehead enjoys a more sustained immunity, though still inherently and tragically unstable, enforced from within. Hers is sexual self-repression in the interest of personal emancipation, not doctrinaire in its expression in the novel but capable of analysis in the context of nineteenth-century feminism.

Sue is a woman seeking self-determination. A strong phase of her personality is contained in the phrase, "I shall do just as I choose!" She often does it, buying the forbidden statues, leaving the school, throwing over Phillotson and Jude turn and turn about. She says she wants "an occupation in which I shall be more independent." She quotes Mill on liberty.

Her model of freedom comes from childhood. However, old Miss Fawley's intriguing account of Sue as a girl pictures her not in the full freedom of infancy but in moments of crucial consciousness of the threats to freedom, so that the childish Sue comes across more as a rebel than a free spirit. She was a good student and accomplished in other ways. "She could do things that only boys do, as a rule." But she was "not exactly a tomboy," partly it seems because she was already aware of gender and its divisions. She would suddenly refuse to play the boys' games. Yet she defied the limits placed on girls. She, who could hit and slide into the pond with the best of the boys, was once cried shame upon by her aunt for wading into that pond with her shoes and stockings off. She answered with twelve-year-old awareness of sexual roles and rebellion against them: "Move on, aunty! This is no sight for modest eyes!"

Jean Brooks is one of the few critics willing to comment on the meaning of Sue's childhood. She compares her infantilism, her longing for childhood, with Catherine Earnshaw's, calling it "a death-wish longing." In my view neither Catherine nor Sue exhibits a death-wish so much as a life-wish. They hark back to a time before the split into sexual and thereby limited beings. Catherine comes to grief by being made a lady of, losing Wuthering Heights, the moors, Heathcliff, her heaven. For an androgynous union as of brother and sister in the panelled bed at the Heights is substituted the division and violence of adult love. Catherine dies in childbirth.

A catalog might be made of brilliant girl children of Victorian literature who stand to lose by growing up and do. Many say that Jane Eyre and Maggie Tulliver are less at their ends than their beginnings. Jane is rather diminished to a happy marriage with her "master." Maggie embraces self-renunciation and death. A classic instance of a fascinating girl's growing up to be a not-very-interesting woman is Pauline Bassompierre in Charlotte Brontë's *Villette*. In the brilliant opening chapters the six-year-old Polly threatens to take the novel away from its heroine, she is so complex, bizarre, above all so individual. But she comes to learn that she must bear a great deal at the hands of men, her father and her eventual husband, because she is a girl. She profits by the lesson, and the result is a happy marriage and the forfeiture of our attention in favor of the unhappy and unmarried Lucy Snowe. One of the most consistently engaging and admirable female characters of Victorian fiction, whose interest lies in her capability, not its defeat, is Alice. She is intelligent, resourceful, strong-minded, aggressive in a polite way that pleases by contrast to the outrageousness of the creatures she meets. She will stand no nonsense at the end of *Wonderland* and wins her game at the end of *Looking-Glass*. Lewis Carroll is often suspiciously regarded for liking little girls. The liking was eccentric insofar as it tended towards exclusiveness, but is it in itself incomprehensible? May not girls have something that they lose in growing up, especially in growing up to be Victorian ladies? Carroll said that he ceased seeing much of a child-friend after about the age of twelve because in most cases she ceased to be interesting. This may be taken as a comment on Carroll or on the girls. It is usually taken the first way, but I think the second way may be equally illuminating. It sheds an indirect light on Sue Bridehead's desire to "get back to the life of my infancy and its freedom," "to remain as I began."

Her method is to remain a virgin. The account of her relationship with the Christminster undergraduate is an important outline of the method. Contact with this young man represents educational "advantages" for Sue, opportunity beyond the usual girl's education. Jude says to her, "you don't talk quite like a girl,—well, a girl who has had no advantages." This is because of her exposure to masculine learning, to books that she would never have gotten hold of without the undergraduate. Sue chooses to be part of a wider world, instead of being cut out of it as out of the boys' games.

In this sense she follows the line of what George Moore calls in his *Drama in Muslin* one of the two representative types of emancipated woman in the later nineteenth century. This is the woman who gravitates toward men more than ever before because masculine contact, in contrast to her constrictive feminine circle, means "light, freedom, and instruction." Yet in another sense Sue belongs to the apparently opposite type of Moore's analysis, the woman who rejects men because of their reduction of women to merely sexual beings. Sue attempts a daring and dangerous combination of gravitation and rejection. This is her method. She says that she owes all of her advantages to a certain peculiarity that has shaped her life. It is that she has no fear of men and can mix with them freely. She removes the sexual barrier by as much as possible removing the sexual element from the relationship. This she does by repressing sexual invitation in herself. "Until [a woman] says by a look 'Come on' he is always afraid to, and if you never say it, or look it, he never comes."

I say that Sue represses her sexuality in an almost deliberate effort at widening her opportunities, but this analysis depends on her having sexual impulses to repress. I think she does, though many would not agree. Gosse says that "the *vita sexualis* of Sue is the central interest of the book," but later critics usually locate the interest in her *lack* of a sexual life. She is often taken at Jude's estimate on those occasions when he calls her sexless, a disembodied creature, incorporeal as a spirit, though it is to be noticed that he takes it all back when, for instance, she shows sexual jealousy over Arabella. Hardy explains in a letter to Gosse that Sue's oddity is sexual in origin, but not perversion and not entire lack. He says that her sexual drive is healthy as far as it goes but weak and fastidious. Michael Steig and Mary Jacobus are in the minority in giving her a significant sexual side. Wayne Burns says that critics have been led astray in denying it by the classic analysis of D. H. Lawrence.

Lawrence finds the woman in Sue Bridehead atrophied. He does not find her completely defunct. However he does assume that she was born thus atrophied, whereas I think it makes a difference that Hardy gives strong evidence of an originally passionate nature self-restrained and so debilitated. This is the force of her purchase of the statues of Venus and Apollo, her reading of Swinburne, her interpretation of the Song of Solomon as a paean to "ecstatic, natural, human love." She says herself that she loves Jude "grossly," and Arabella, who knows about these things, has the last word in the novel when she says Sue will never find peace outside of Jude's arms. It is true that Hardy's picture of Sue's sexual basis is so complex that it sometimes seems contradictory. For instance, one perplexing passage says she is "unfitted by temperament and instinct to fulfill the conditions of the matrimonial relation with

Phillotson, possibly with scarce any man." This seems to imply inborn coldness; but then again is it sexual relations as such that instinct unfits her for, or their conditions, that is, their enforced nature in marriage? Also the ambiguity of the "possibly" is increased by the fact that two pages before Sue has kissed "close and long" with Jude, running spontaneously to meet his embrace and leaving it with "flushed cheeks."

I think when Hardy describes Sue at the Melchester School as "a woman clipped and pruned by severe discipline, an under-brightness shining through from the depths which that discipline had not yet been able to reach," we may understand both the under-brightness and the discipline as sexual in nature. Central to the treatment of the Training School is its powerful but repressed sexual charge. But unlike the other young women's discipline, Sue's is not only externally laid on. Hers is also a matter of herself neither saying or looking "Come on." The likeliest way to accomplish this over the long run would be to stop *feeling* "Come on."

A number of critics say that beneath her unconventionality Sue is really conventional. Heilman and Emmett call her sexual standoffishness a giveaway of ordinary Victorian prudishness. Millett suggests the same thing. But it is not ordinary. There was more than one tradition of female chastity. The ordinary one may be represented by the rule in Charlotte Yonge's complete Victorian lady's guide, *Womankind*—that a young lady must exercise self-restraint since "in almost all men there is a worse part which makes them willing to incite a girl to go as far as she will with them, and is flattered at the approaches to indiscretion which all the time make her forfeit their respect." Less ordinary is the specialized version of certain feminists. In fact Victorian feminists were responding to the same thing that Victorian prudes were—the noticeable disadvantages of being seen in a sexual light by men.

It is a commonplace of male literary treatment of emancipated women in the century to picture them like Tennyson's Princess Ida, walled off from the masculine world in a sort of convent-college of militant chastity, over whose gates stands written, death to any man that enters. It is a scientific commonplace to infer, like Herbert Spencer, flatchestedness in intellectually advanced women. The image of the new woman who rejects men appears often in the journals, for instance in the anti-feminist *Saturday Review*, which in an article of 1896 opposes the granting of university degrees to women because "it ministers to the new aspiration of some women for 'living their own lives'—that is, in fact, getting rid of the fetters of matrimony and maternity." I will cite George Moore again on this emancipated type:

> women who in the tumult of their aspirations, and their pas
> sionate yearnings towards the new ideal, and the memory of
> the abasement their sex have in the past, and still are being
> in the present, subjected to, forget the laws of life, and with
> virulent virtue and protest, condemn love—that is to say, love
> in the sense of sexual intercourse—and claim a higher mission
> for woman than to be the mother of men.

There may be a question whether this reflects mainly masculine presuppositions or new women as they actually lived and thought. This is also the question where Hardy gets Sue. We should turn to what some of the feminists themselves said.

A classic illustration of feminist ambivalence about sex is Mary Wollstonecraft's *Vindication of the Rights of Women*. Wollstonecraft lavishes outrage on the demeaning of women as the sexual objects of men, so that their whole training is towards the arts of enticement at the expense of every other reasonable human endeavor. Wollstonecraft was herself a passionate woman, tempestuous even; she attempted suicide twice for deserted love. She expresses as little attraction to the Houyhnhnms as the Yahoos. She defends healthy physicality in women—an appetite that is not puny and ladylike, unconstrained exercise in sport, dancing even to the point of hot faces and sweat. "Women as well as men ought to have the common appetites and passions of their nature, they are only brutal when unchecked by reason." But the point is that they ought to be checked. A heavy emphasis of the *Vindication* is to devalue passionate love. It is a romantic interlude and not the sine qua non, to be made the object of a woman's whole life. Wollstonecraft insists on the extremely short life of passion, cooled in weeks or months to be replaced by rational married comradeship. "In a great degree, love and friendship cannot subsist in the same bosom." She is in a hurry to get to the friendly stage and to dilate on its virtues. "A master and mistress of a family ought not to continue to love each other with passion." Since Wollstonecraft and virtually all feminists after her lay the blame for a woman's oppression and incapacity on her rearing first and foremost as man's sexual object, it is no wonder that many of them feel some reservation about sexuality, at the very least demoting it from the top rank of importance. So Wollstonecraft devotes a chapter to modesty, she praises Diana, she is disgusted by women's habits of bodily intimacy, she is very sensible of the "gross" and "nasty," and sounds distinctly puritanical. She does not denounce motherhood. In fact she says it is a woman's noblest function and that instead of being trained for the harem she should be trained for the nursery. But a number of later feminists wanted to escape both. For instance, in her *Morality of Marriage* Mona Caird says, "the gardener takes care that his very peach-trees and rose-bushes shall not be weakened by overproduction . . . valuable animals are spared in the same way and for the same reason. It is only women for whom there is no mercy." She asks, "do we not see that the mother of half a dozen children, who struggles to cultivate her faculties, to be an intelligent human being, nearly always breaks down under the burden, or shows very marked intellectual limitations?" Such feminists had twice as much reason for sharing Wollstonecraft's low estimation of sex, and their position helps to explain Sue Bridehead.

A valuable book by J. A. and Olive Banks treats later nineteenth-century feminist doctrine as part of an investigation of *Feminism and Family Planning in Victorian England*. Its discussion of feminists' sexual attitudes helps explain their silence on birth control, controversial in the 1870s. The Banks conclude that silence meant non-support, the reason being suspicion of contraceptive methods for offering further sexual license to men, to which women owed so much of their oppression. Feminist journals like the *Englishwoman's Journal,* the *Englishwoman's Review,* and the *Victorian Magazine* were not silent on another controversial issue of the 1870s and 1880s. This was Josephine Butler's campaign against the Contagious Diseases Act, which took prostitutes under state regulation and enforced their medical examination in order to stem the spread of venereal disease. The Act was seen by most feminists as condoning the double standard by treating men's philandering as a venial sin, a mere hygiene problem. The law was considered offensive since it detained prostitutes while their customers went free, and offered no guarantee against indiscriminate detention. The Banks illustrate the feminist position by citing a speech in favor of the Act's repeal that attacks "the assumption that indulgence is a necessity of man." The attitude held after the Act fell. A writer in the early twentieth-century *Freewoman* finds "sex-intercourse—otherwise subjection to man" and concludes that "women are forced to crush down sex, but in doing so, they are able to use the greatest dynamic, passion, for the liberation of women." According to the feminists, the solution to the problem of venereal disease, among other problems, was chastity for men, as women already practiced it. The Banks sum up this line of thought with the suffragist slogan, "Votes for Women and Purity for Men." One of their most bizarre evidences of feminist antagonism to sexuality is a poem by Ellis Ethelmer, "Woman Free" of 1893, which looks to the equalization of the sexes for respite from menstruation by removal of its cause, men's undue sexual demands on women.

Some did support both contraception and women's rights. George Drysdale's *Elements of Social Science, or Physical, Sexual, and Natural Religion* argues the benefit of "venereal exercise" for women and men alike, to be enjoyed without Malthusian disaster by the use of birth control. He says that maladies of sexual frustration are in fact worse for a woman (from iron deficient blood to hysteria). She needs relief even more than a man because she is, under "our unfortunate social arrangements," far more dependent on love than man." We can see the feminism in the phrase "unfortunate social arrangements," and also foresee the parting of the ways between him and other feminists. His argument for sexual fulfillment partly concedes to the "unfortunate social arrangements" that make a woman's life destitute without it. The opposite tack is to minimize the need for love so as to reduce women's dependence on men in this as in other ways. The latter line of thought represents the feminist mainstream according to the Banks.

Feminist uneasiness about sex could be more or less encompassing. A review would have to include in addition to Wollstonecraft's asceticism, Margaret Fuller's denial of the Byronic axiom that love is a woman's whole existence and her glorification of virginity in *Woman in the Nineteenth Century,* and Christabel Pankhurst's salvaging in *The Great Scourge and How to End It* of the one valuable lesson—chastity—from women's history of subjection. J. S. Mill identifies the wife's duty of submission to her husband's desire as the ultimate form of slavery.

Hardy explicitly says in a letter to Gosse what he felt he must leave circumspectly implied in his novel, that part of Sue's reluctance to marry is her reluctance to relinquish the right to "withhold herself at pleasure, or altogether." This is behind Sue's aversion to being "licensed to be loved on the premises." As Fernando points out, the link between women's rights and the right over one's own body expressed in withholding it casts Sue in a distinctly feminist light.

Certainly she speaks of sex and marriage as the opposite of freedom. When she finally sleeps with Jude it is giving in, being conquered, being caught. She doesn't want to have children. She wishes "some harmless mode of vegetation might have peopled Paradise." A bride, to her, is the heifer brought to the sacrifice. Jude reflects this attitude when he greets her, newly married to Phillotson, as a woman still free, with an individuality *not yet* squashed and digested by wifedom.

Living fifteen months with her undergraduate friend, Sue remains as she began. Jude congratulates her on her innocence, but she responds rather unexpectedly. She says that she is not particularly innocent. In fact, she has a bad conscience about her method. She says a "better woman" would not have held off. Sue is uneasy about her inhibition of sexuality. This ambivalence again shows her distance from merely ordinary attitudes on female purity. Neither is she a feminist programmatically heart-whole in her principles because she is simultaneously a believer in "ecstatic, natural, human love."

Her division roughly reflects the division in feminist theory, which had its hedonist along with its stronger ascetic impulse. For instance, Wollstonecraft's writings after the *Vindication* show her recognition of the strength of female passion, however heavily fraught with problems, and there were a few true erotic enthusiasts among the advocates of free love discussed by Hal Sears in *The Sex Radicals, Free Love in High Victorian America,* though the larger number of them stressed a woman's right of refusal, restraint, abstinence, continence, and varieties of quite stringent sublimation. A good spokesman for the feminism of erotic liberation is Edmund d'Auvergne in the *Freewoman.* Where Christabel Pankhurst endorses chastity in the cause of women, d'Auvergne finds it a male imposition and thinks Penelope should have enjoyed herself with the suitors as Odysseus did with Circe and Calypso.

"Better women" would have slept with their house-mates. Though it seems to be altogether necessary, holding out is not altogether good, which is why Sue Bridehead reflects about her life with the undergraduate, "men are—so much better than women!" There is an irony in her method of liberation. It allows her to mingle freely with men and to share their advantages, eliminating the barrier of gender by as much as possible eliminating gender. Sue is "almost as one of their own sex." Almost but not quite. It is significant that she is described as boyish, dressed in Jude's clothes, a Ganymede. The liberating strategy makes her in a sense a boy rather than a man. It rules out exactly that aspect of masculinity that makes men "better."

Throughout the novel Sue suffers oddly excessive guilt culminating in her desire at the end to prick herself all over with pins to bleed the badness out. I think the double source of her bad conscience can be traced to her relation with the undergraduate which prefigures that with

Jude. She combines Moore's two types of liberation, to live with men and to escape them. This program involves injury to herself and to the man. She stunts her own nature and frustrates her lover.

There is evidence that Sue knows that sexual repression means loss as well as gain. She is defensive against people's idea that she is sexless— "I won't have it!" On occasion she seems to regret her coldness, even to Phillotson—"I am so cold, or devoid of gratitude, or so something." She suspects that Jude will hold her in "contempt" for not loving Phillotson as a husband. She feels some "shamefacedness" at letting Phillotson know of her incomplete relations with Jude. She shows herself the reverse of proud when she says, "I know I am a poor miserable creature. My nature is not so passionate as yours." She knows she makes others miserable as well. She helps kill the undergraduate, wounds Phillotson in career and spirit, tortures Jude—"O I seem so bad—upsetting men's courses like this!"

Sue attempts a compromise. But to mitigate the first sort of injury is the more certainly to impose the other. That is, the more she allows her sexual nature to survive in self-protective permutations, the more vulnerable she makes her lover. Bad conscience is a distinguishing feature of her attempt to live a free woman. The compromise is essentially Platonic in theory, or more specifically Shelleyan. She enunciates it in the passage on her life with the undergraduate. "Some of the most passionately erotic poets have been the most self-contained in their daily lives." This justifies both eroticism and self-containment. It is a doctrine of sublimation quite Freudian in its assumption of the importance of sexual drive to higher mental or spiritual attainments. Implied also is the perpetuation of the drive by obstacle and deflection, so that it is not quelled by satiation. This idea runs all through Hardy, as brilliantly demonstrated by J. Hillis Miller in *Thomas Hardy, Distance and Desire*. The theory of augmenting desire by distance gives Sue part of her brief against marriage. If married people were forbidden each other's embrace instead of locked into it by contract, she says, "there'd be little cooling then!"

The concrete illustration of Sue's Platonic/Shelleyan love theory is her fondness for windows. Her escape from the Training School window seems to represent sexual liberation, since she goes to Jude's lodging, but the jump from Phillotson's bedroom window represents quite another kind, one which Jude comes to experience himself in a milder version when Sue sends him to sleep by himself. The two modes resolve into Sue's favorite disposition of the sexes, making spiritual love with a window in between. Jude and Sue have a tender talk through a window at Marygreen, and their interview at Shaston becomes more tender once Jude is outside the casement. She says, "'I can talk to you better like this than when you were inside' . . . Now that the high window-sill was between them, so that he could not get at her."

If Sue's project for liberation is in good part one of inhibited sexuality, it by no means aims at total extirpation, or total rejection of men. The reasons are that she needs men for the advantage they offer, the undergraduate's books, for instance, and just as important, she needs them for their sexual stimulus. This sounds paradoxical for the repressive Sue, but the more repressed she is, the more stimulus does she need, for sublimation must have something to work on. I think Lawrence shows the finest insight of anyone who has written on Sue Bridehead when he says that she needs Jude to arouse the atrophied female in her, so as to stimulate the brightness of her mind.

Jude calls her a flirt, which she is, and the novel is a classic formulation of flirt psychology, all the more remarkable for linking the flirt to the feminist. If we think these roles mutually exclusive, as Cockshut does, we are cast back on the idea that Sue is not a new woman but an ordinary old one after all. This misses a lot. Heilman's is a good analysis of Sue as coquette. He observes that the coquette wants to attract and yet remain unobtainable. He gives the reason that she needs to exert power. It seems to me that this is validly observed from a man's point of view, Jude's say, who feels his helplessness under a woman's sway, and it may be part of the picture on the woman's side too. It is commonly said that flirts use men, but less commonly said what they use them *for*. I think a great deal of Sue's use of men comes from her feminist double bind. She needs to keep alive in herself a sexuality in danger of being disciplined all the way down to the source.

Men may feel that a woman triumphs in the power of frigidity by remaining untouchable while making a man know his own vulnerability, but it should also be understood that she may freeze in her own cold. She may need, even desperately, for a man to warm her. Masculine impotence is widely understood to spawn in the sufferer psychological complications of the most fascinating pathos. Feminine impotence is usually understood as the man's suffering more than the woman's. But Hardy goes a great deal beyond the usual, that is, beyond the masculine perspective. He shows the impulse behind Sue's "love of being loved," which is the more insatiable for her own difficulty in loving. This impulse owes less to the power of the strong than to the need of the much weakened.

In *Jude the Obscure,* more than in any of his other novels, Hardy investigates the potential liability of the doctrine of distance and desire, that is, of desire stretched to farther and farther distances from direct satisfaction, so that it begins to attenuate, until it is in danger of losing itself. The novel also examines what such a loss would mean. Sue Bridehead is like a reinvestigation from the inside of Marty South of *The Woodlanders,* published seven years before. Marty and Giles Winterborne enjoy the most serene love in the book because it dispenses with sex. In *Jude* Hardy still depicts passion as virulent, and so Sue defends herself against it. But the novel also shows, intimately, dismayingly, what it would mean to try to be like Marty South, "a being who had rejected with indifference the attribute of sex for the loftier quality of abstract humanism."

Sue's inhibition of sexuality, though not beyond her uneasy consciousness, is beyond her control. Hardy shows that it is there to be drawn out, but only if Jude takes the initiative. "By every law of nature and sex a kiss was the only rejoinder that fitted the mood and the moment, under the suasion of which Sue's undemonstrative regard of him might not inconceivably have changed its temperature." He does not kiss her, and his acquiescence in her sexlessness reinforces it in her.

However, her attenuated sexual nature does remain alive in alternative and bizarre forms. There is her jealousy, which proves to Jude that she is not, after all, a sexless creature. There is her disgust, which she cherishes in an odd way. The only thing worse than her shrinking from Phillotson would be to get used to him, for then it would be "like saying that the amputation of a limb is no affliction, since a person gets comfortably accustomed to the use of a wooden leg or arm in the course of time!" To feel repugnance is at least not to accept being an amputee. The oddest form of Sue's rerouted sexuality is her device of provoking pain in order to feel pity, as when she makes Jude walk up the church aisle with her just before she is to marry Phillotson. She later says that her relation to Jude began in the wish to make his heart ache for her without letting hers ache for him. But Hardy shows that her feeling is really much more complicated. In fact, Sue goes out of her way to induce in herself pain, long-suffering, and pity. In so doing she is "an epicure in emotions," satisfying her "curiosity to hunt up a new sensation." Far from triumphing in lack of feeling, Sue strains after sensation of some sort. Since she does not feel desire directly, she invents original and "perverse" substitutes.

A curious technique for stimulating sensation in herself is to pose obstacles which will produce pain, which she can then pity. What makes this curious is that the obstacles are sometimes social conventions that she does not believe in. For instance, she plans to punish Jude by letter for making her give way to an unconventional impulse and allow a kiss. Of course she is usually highly unconventional, on both the subject of religion and the subject of marriage, so that in theory it should not matter to her that the future parson kisses a woman who is not his wife. Yet she turns around to make it matter, according to the extraordinary logic that "things that were right in theory were wrong in practice." This is not simple illogic but a quite orderly psychological maneuver for the production of sentiment: "Tears of pity for Jude's approaching sufferings at her hands mingled with those which had surged up in pity for herself."

It is important to understand Sue's unexpected invocations of convention. These have led some to think hers an unconventionality of the surface only; according to this interpretation her prostration to the letter of the law at the end is simply a true showing of the ordinary stuff she has been made of all along. A woman's succumbing to convention is a repeated idea in Hardy, as in "The Elopement": "in time convention won her, as it wins all women at last." He gives several explanations for Sue's succumbing. One does support the view that she has a conventional stratum to fall back on, when courage or reason fails, or circumstances become too strong. That is, Phillotson explains her return to the idea of the indissolubility of marriage by her soaking in Christminster sentiment and teaching, in spite of all she has said against them. There is in this sense some credence to Lawrence's analysis that Sue is the product of ages of Christianity in spite of her proclaimed paganism. Sue herself often blames her timidity for the breakdown of her theoretic unorthodoxy. Jude questions whether the demise of her advanced views is accountable to a defect in women's reason: "Is a woman a thinking unit at all?" Later he attributes the narrowing of her views to the way that "time and circumstances" operate on women. Hardy seems to accept Jude's idea of "strange difference of sex"; he calls women "The Weaker" himself. But in what sense weaker? Of course one way of answering would be as Jude implies, that men's views enlarge while women's narrow in adversity because men are made of stronger stuff. Another way of answering would be, less that men are stronger than that "time and circumstances" are less strong against them, which turns out to be the case in the novel. "The woman mostly gets the worst of it, in the long run!" says Jude. "She does," says Sue.

In giving so many accounts of what weakens Sue, Hardy comes across as less dogmatic than any isolated passage may suggest. He is true, in the aggregate, to a complexity in her character beyond the simple explanations that he has his characters, as it were, try out on her. Above all, he shows that even when Sue appears to act conventionally, she often does so out of the most unconventional of motives. This makes inadequate the idea that she exposes at the end an ordinariness that has only been covered over with daring theories. Sue may be overpowered, she may fall short of her promise, she may buckle to the letter of the law, but she is never ordinary. Just as her sexual repression comes from her feminism, more than from the Victorian commonplace of feminine purity which it externally resembles, so does much of her behavior represent tactics in a highly individualized feminist program, sometimes just when it looks the most externally conventional.

We have seen how Sue uses convention unconventionally to induce sensation. Another way she uses it is to shield herself from sex, for reasons very much her own, as we have also seen. For instance, she goes to visit Phillotson in his illness after she has left him. He shows signs of warming from friend to husband, and Sue, in her "incipient fright" shows herself ready to seize on "*any line of defense* against marital feelings in him" (my emphasis). She claims her own wickedness in leaving, so that he can't possibly want her back. There is no question of her believing this; she grasps at it willy-nilly. Another instance of Sue's self-defense with any odd weapon that comes to hand is her tortured reasoning to show why she cannot marry Jude. She invokes the letter of the law in its very finest print. Her argument goes like this: since she did not commit adultery with Jude, her divorce from Phillotson was obtained under false pretenses; it is no divorce, so she cannot marry Jude, which she clearly does not want to do for personal reasons quite other than legal.

Sue's contradictoriness has depth and coherence. It represents an impressively original experiment in life and freedom. It also fails of its own divisions. Lawrence comes closest to explaining how this is, though his explanation must be disentangled from his sometimes offensive definitions of what it means to be a woman or a man, and from his idea that Sue was born with an unhealthy overbalance of the masculine. He recognizes that Hardy is concerned with something more complex than the pioneer's defeat by the simple retribution of an outraged society. He proposes the analysis that the pioneer breaks down through inability to bear the isolation. But I think he goes beyond this too, by suggesting that Sue's breakdown inheres in her very method of pioneering. He says,

"It was a cruelly difficult position. . . . She wanted some quickening for this atrophied female. She wanted even kisses. That the new rousing might give her a sense of life. But she could only *live* in the mind. . . . She could only receive the highest stimulus, which she must inevitably seek, from a man who put her in constant jeopardy."

This accords with my own view. Sue's method of emancipation is sexual repression, but by no means total repudiation of sex or men. In addition to wanting what men have to offer intellectually, she needs men to keep alive the driving force of feeling, sexual at its root, recognized as essential in her Platonic/Shelleyan theory of sublimation. A man stimulates her sexual nature, which she directs into relatively safe channels, jealousy, disgust, and epicurean emotions, thereby evading the worst of the "inexorable laws of nature" for women. But the safety is precarious because the man must feel desire direct, to satisfy her "love of being loved." He is always there with his desire, reminding her of the comparative debility of her own, and of the injury she causes in leaving him unsatisfied. She feels guilt on both counts. She feels herself a kind of stand-out to the life force which she values and needs in him, even though she knows it would also sweep her away from her individuality and her freedom. The man is always there, always insisting, which she wants, but he is also blaming her, as it is clear Jude does. In spite of his protestations of love to her as an incarnate spirit, when he sees his chance, he presses for what he really wants by complaining of the "poor returns" he gets from her on his love. Using Arabella's reappearance he pressures Sue into sleeping with him. Her balance is precarious because it rests upon a difference between what she feels and what Jude feels, a difference at the same time necessary to her purposes and dangerous to them. She "gives in," she sleeps with him, and the balance is upset.

Yet Sue and Jude are happy together for a certain unspecified number of years. Hardy moves very quickly over this period, which leaves some readers in doubt of their happiness. Neither Lawrence nor Heilman can believe that Sue could have adjusted to a normal sexual relationship. Though the picture remains sketchy, I think it is important for an interpretation of Sue to take Hardy at his word: "that the twain were happy—between their times of sadness—was indubitable." Sue's reservation is overcome, as charmingly symbolized by Jude's pushing her face into the roses at the Great Wessex Agricultural Show, which she had thought the rules prohibited her to touch. "'Happy?' he murmured. She nodded."

The flower scene represents a return to "Greek joyousness." Sue explains later that they lived according to a new theory of nature—to

"make a virtue of joy . . . be joyful in what instincts she afforded us."
She says that with whatever coolness on her side her relation with Jude
began, she did get to love him after Arabella's arrival pushed them
together, and that this love is passionate we gather from the way she
returns his kisses even after she has renounced him to return to Phillotson. Arabella notices that if she is cooler than Jude, "she cares for
him pretty middling much." Sue is able to love and she does. She puts
her Platonic theory behind her and lives for a time by a new code. Yet
Hardy shows that the self-protectiveness of the old code was against real
dangers, which descend upon Sue when she abandons it, making her
revert to an extreme version of the sexual renunciation which had been
her original position. But now instead of being self-creative, it is self-
destructive.

The liability of love is made flesh in children. Sue is not ashamed
of her passion during her happy time with Jude, especially since she still
protects her freedom from being married and licensed to be loved on the
premises. But she does question the result of passion. Since the woman
bears the children, she bears the question more heavily. This is especially
true for this pair, since Sue has more of herself—a star to Jude's benzoline
lamp—to lose. When Father Time first calls Sue mother, she begins to
feel herself "getting intertwined with my kind." She feels she must give
over "struggling against the current." Sue is someone who had tried to
live by Mill's doctrine—"who lets the world, or his own portion of it,
choose his plan of life for him, has no need of any other faculty than
the ape-like one of imitation.'" For her, to give up the struggle is to give
up her higher faculties. The children make compromise necessary, to
which Sue and Jude add compromise on the compromise, so that they
give up some of their own freedom without providing their family complete respectability. They can laugh when Jude is fired for carving the
ten commandments while breaking the seventh, but laughter is less possible when looking for lodgings for a family of five when the landlady
wants to know, "Are you really a married woman?" Sue must either be
true to her principles by saying she isn't, or to her children by saying
she is. Given the social structure, children represent a conflict between
personal liberty and concession to one's kind. But Hardy goes beyond
blaming society. Sue says, "it seems such a terribly tragic thing to bring
beings into the world—so presumptuous—that I question my right to
do it sometimes!" Her guilt at bearing children seems well-founded in
view of the Hardy world that awaits them—in Phillotson's summary,
"cruelty is the law pervading all nature and society." The joy-in-instinct

theory of nature by which Sue had tried to live is revealed as partial through the crucial episode of little Father Time's murder/suicide.

Father Time is so broadly symbolic that he is rather hard to take and hard to pin down. What makes him, for one thing, Sue's and Jude's "nodal point, their focus, their expression in a single term"? Does he enact the interior necessity of their love's disruption and Sue's about-face, or is he only one of Hardy's supernumeraries of nemesis? I think the catastrophe he brings about is not coincidental, because he acts out what Sue already feels, that she should not have had children. Having them is something she tells little Jude she must be "forgiven" for. Sue explains that a "law of nature" brought them to birth, and in killing them and himself he repudiates this law of nature.

Sue had originally sought to sidestep the law, before rather than after the fact. Then for a time she had allowed herself to imagine that the law is joy-in-instinct. But it turns out to be the inexorable law of nature, as it is called in the early passage on the women students. Women live out this law intimately, in their own bodies, and it means "injustice, loneliness, child-bearing, and bereavement." "The woman gets the worst of it." Jude blames himself for having disrupted the precarious equilibrium of their relationship, which had allowed evasion of the worst of nature's law. Sue agrees that she should have remained as she began. Circumstances have persuaded her that she was right in her original position.

Hardy seems to support by the catastrophic fact Sue's analysis that "there is something external to us which says, 'you shan't,'" including "'you shan't love.'" However precarious, there seems to be some reasonableness in her original attempt to evade this external "you shan't" by means of an internally imposed "you shan't." The latter allows a semblance of volition and self-determination which harnesses instinct to safer ends, at least, than hanging.

Sue's reaction to the decimation of her family is understandable. It is a return to an extreme form of her original position, self-mastery, self-renunciation. But no longer does she try to control her fate; she places it utterly outside her own hands. She now wishes to "mortify the flesh, the terrible flesh—the curse of Adam." This sounds like the sexual repression she started out with, except that then she never denied the force for possible good of sexuality. The contrast can be seen in that before she counted men "better" for their desire, while at the end she counts women "superior" for never instigating, only responding. Before she had thought that instinct could be made the drivewheel of personal development. She had not wanted to accept amputation and was glad even of disgust as a sign that the flesh could still feel its loss. The burning of the nightgown worn with Jude and the forcing of her nature to go to Phillotson represent, in contrast, a terribly complete amputation.

In trying at the end to utterly eradicate instinct in herself, she gives up all forward motion. She says she wants to die in childbirth. Spiritually, she makes her sexual nature into death, whereas before in its paradoxical way it had been life. So Sue is described as a person bereft of will. She is "cowed," feels "creeping paralysis." "I have no more fighting strength left, no more enterprise." "All initiatory power seemed to have left her." Self-suppression is now "despairing."

Hardy says in a letter to Florence Henniker, "seriously I don't see any possible scheme for the union of the sexes that w[ou]ld be satisfactory." This attitude turns *Jude* into something quite different from a social-problem novel, since the problem goes deeper than society. It renders doubtful much optimism for what might have been had Sue and Jude not been fifty years before their time. The law of nature would still remain. To inhibit nature is not the answer. It causes some loss and some guilt. It also doesn't work very well, since instinct cannot be totally stultified if it is to remain at call for redirection. The love of being loved is actually a clamoring need. Instinct must feed on the stimulus of a lover's direct desire, with all the disequilibrium that implies. But to act on natural impulse is not the answer either. The law of nature is "inexorable," and procreation brings guilt and retribution both. Sue's precarious balance is an impressive experiment in self-creation. The experiment might have continued to work after its fashion, but the internal pressure is great, so that it is no surprise or final blame to her when the upset comes.

The German reviewer whom Hardy credits in his preface with calling Sue "the woman of the feminist movement," also says that if she had been created by a woman she would never have been allowed to break down at the end. Not all who say that Hardy is great on women say that he is kind to them. Lascelles Abercrombie calls his treatment "subtle, a little cruel, not as tolerant as it seems." He often shows a woman character weak, changeable, and in the wrong, and he is quick, often distressingly so (the earlier the novel the more distressingly) to generalize from the woman to women, while the man is allowed to represent only himself. He characterizes women straightforwardly as "The Weaker" in *Jude*. However, I do not think this weakness comes across in the richly detailed portrait of Sue Bridehead as weakness in animal force, intellect, drive, venturesomeness, originality, or accomplishment. The explanations Hardy offers for her weakness become less definitive as they multiply. If *Jude* sometimes seems a paradise of loose ends, in Arthur Mizener's nice phrase, I think it never seems more so than when we hear that Sue's collapse comes from her indoctrination in conventions, or that women lack courage, or is it reason, or is it that they contract as men expand? No doubt a woman author, that is, a feminist woman author, would not have had Sue break down for these reasons. But I don't think they are Hardy's essential reasons either.

Rather in Sue Bridehead he dramatizes a daring and plausible try at personal liberation which runs into problems, reflective of the times but by no means yet altogether superseded, that a woman gains freedom as she gains access to a man's wider world while ceasing to be his sexual object. Sue sets about to mix with men freely, but neither to say or look or feel "Come on," rather to redirect that impulse to safer channels. But once the premise is acted on, she runs afoul of universal law, which touches women so closely, and which dictates that if it is dangerous to act naturally, so is it dangerous to inhibit nature. Sue's breakdown is not a judgment on her. It is a judgment on the way things are between the sexes according to Hardy, and that is a war that probably can't be won.

Jude the Obscure: Reading and the Spirit of the Law

Ramón Saldívar

> The letter killeth, but the spirit giveth life.
> 2 CORINTHIANS

Concern for the nature and response of an author's audience is, in some respects, one of the original tasks of literary criticism. Over the past decade, however, attempts to incorporate rhetorical, linguistic, and cognitive theories into literary criticism have led to the development of a hefty bibliography on the nature of the reader's role in the communication network of author, text, and reader. These reader-oriented studies stress, from their various perspectives, that the reader, as much as any character, contributes to the shaping of the novel's fictive world through his interpretive actions.

The value of this recent emphasis on the reader's role in fiction and of "reception history" in general could very well be tested by a text such as the author's "Postscript" to *Jude the Obscure*. There, the reading public is accused of "curing" the novelist of all desire to write prose fiction. In this case Hardy would seem to have us question the reader's role in the *destruction* of texts, for in no uncertain terms, it is the reader, in his incapacity to read, who is the problem. Since we cannot read his meaning properly, even when there has been no "mincing of words" in its enunciation, complains Hardy, he will spare himself and the reader by simply ceasing to write novels.

Yet readers often find this and Hardy's later comment that he expected *Jude the Obscure* to be read as "a moral work" somewhat disingenuous. We can hardly imagine, after the reception of *Tess* and after his

---

From *ELH* 50, no. 3 (1983). © 1983 by the Johns Hopkins University Press.

attempt to cancel his contract with Harper & Brothers for *Jude,* that Hardy would not have anticipated the "shocked criticisms" that the publication of the novel evoked. In fact, when Hardy announces in the "Preface to the First Edition" that the novel will "deal unaffectedly with the fret and fever, derision and disaster, that may press in the wake of the strongest passion known to humanity," and then denies that "there is anything in the handling to which exception can be taken," he raises the very real possibility that the novel will be misread.

And it was misread. Angry reviewers and a solemn bishop saw in it, among other things, a cynical attack on the sacrament and institution of marriage. In a letter of November 1895 to Edmund Gosse, Hardy continued to express his concern for the proper reading of his novel by indicating that *Jude* was not merely "a manifesto on 'the marriage question' (although, of course, it involves it)," but was more the story of the tragic result of two marriages because of "a doom or curse of hereditary temperament peculiar to the family of the parties." The fact is, of course, as critics have convincingly argued, that the novel *is* concerned with the marriage laws in more than just a casual way. And Hardy himself points out that the plot of *Jude* is "geometrically constructed" around the marital realignments of the four principal characters. They repeatedly change their relationships through their alternately prospective and restrospective visions of one another and of the options society and nature allow them.

Poised between a desire for natural freedom and the need for a stabilizing social order, Hardy's characters try to act within their "geometrically constructed" system of marital and symbolic associations to accommodate their desires and needs. Hardy is clear about this. He tells us that *Jude the Obscure* dramatizes the sociological effect of the Victorian failure to reconcile the antithetical realms of culture and nature: "The marriage laws [are] used . . . to show that, in Diderot's words, the civil law should be only the enunciation of the law of nature" ("Postscript"). But the difficulty of reading *Jude* properly may well stem from the fact that the novel is more than a realistic analysis of the historical condition of marriage in late Victorian England. I would like to suggest that the ambiguous status of the act of reading in the author's prefatory statements is only an indicator of a more radical investigation concerning reading and interpretation. By considering the interplay between "natural" and "civil" law, and by examining the nature of Hardy's "geometrically constructed" plot, we will be able to reflect on the possible relation of these issues to the apparent ease with which, according to

Hardy, the novel can be misread. A reading of *Jude* that attempts to account for this cluster of formal and thematic elements can, I think, provide a new perspective on Hardy's conception of the realistic novel.

A first difficulty in understanding the novel is thematic and stems from the portrayal in the text itself of numerous cases of misreading. From the beginning, for instance, Jude sees in Christminster and its university the image of an attainable ideal world. His desire for this ideal vision involves a rejection of reality. For his own sporadically controlled, partially understood world, he substitutes the image of a unified, stable, and understandable one. Beguiled by his desire for order, the young Jude thus turns initially to language study both as a means of entering university life and as a possible course of stability. The narrator tells us:

> Ever since his first ecstasy or vision of Christminster and its
> possibilities, Jude had meditated much and curiously on the
> probable sort of process that was involved in turning the
> expressions of one language into those of another. He con-
> cluded that a grammar of the required tongue would contain,
> primarily, a rule, prescription, or clue of the nature of a secret
> cipher which, once known, would enable him, by merely
> applying it, to change at will all words of his own speech
> into those of the foreign one. . . . Thus he assumed that the
> words of the required language were always to be found
> somewhere latent in the words of the given language by those
> who had the art to uncover them, such art being furnished
> by the books aforesaid.
>
> (part 1, ch. 4)

Jude feels betrayed, consequently, when in his attempt to learn Latin he finds that "there was no law of transmutation, as in his innocence he had supposed." Jude's desired "law of transmutation," the "secret cipher" to a system of translation, could exist only if a prior permanent code existed to allow a free substitution of signifiers for one autonomous signified. The metaphor of translation at this early point in the novel is doubly interesting. It both reveals Jude's desire for a serenely immobile text whose content might be transported without harm into the element of another language, and alludes to the relation Hardy establishes in the "Postscript" of 1912 between civil and natural law, making one the "enunciation" of the other. These will continue to be decisive issues throughout the novel. At this point, Jude has no doubt that the voice of nature can, indeed, be read and translated, for when he "address[es] the breeze caressingly," it seems to respond: "Suddenly there came along this wind something towards him—a message . . . calling to him, 'We are happy here!'" (part 1, ch. 3). By imposing single terms on the disparate variety of experience, we come to know and control our environment. Early on, however, Jude intuits that language is not a fixed system through which meaning can be "transmuted" from one system to another. Yet this is precisely the insight that Jude refuses to apply to his other readings of the world around him.

As he proceeds into the countryside, where the markings that hint at the limitations already imposed on his life stand to be deciphered, Jude's readings continue: "The only marks on the uniformity of the scene were a rick of last year's produce . . . and the path . . . by which he had come. . . . [To] every clod and stone there really attached associations enough and to spare—echoes of songs . . . of spoken words, and of sturdy deeds" (part 1, ch. 2). History, echoing across the generations, seems to focus on Jude at the bottom of "this vast concave" field (part 1, ch. 2), but he does not yet understand its voice. The substance of this discourse latent in the countryside is the essential dimension of the tradition into which he has been born. These "marks" and "associations" in the landscape of Wessex are "signs" inscribed by the force motivating all events, which Hardy was in *The Dynasts* to name the "Immanent Will." Thus, long before his birth, long before the story of his family has been inscribed, this tradition has already traced the pattern of behavior within which are ordered the possible changes and exchanges that will occur in Jude's short life. Each crucial event in Jude's life seems to invite the reader to interpret Jude's actions as an attempted reading of the role ascribed to him in some determining book of fate.

Initially, the young orphan Jude seems to see the schoolmaster, Phillotson, as an embodiment of his controlling "dreams" (part 1, ch. 3), and as a symbolic substitute for the absent "real" father. Accordingly, when Phillotson leaves Marygreen, Jude replaces him with an ideal representation. Jude reads that ideal presence into the natural landscape of Wessex as Christminster, "that ecclesiastical romance in stone" (part 1, ch. 5):

> Through the solid barrier of cold cretaceous upland to the northward he was always beholding a gorgeous city—the fancied place he likened to the new Jerusalem. . . . And the city acquired a tangibility, a permanence, a hold on his life, mainly from the one nucleus of fact that the man for whose knowledge

and purposes he had so much reverence was actually living there.

(part 1, ch. 3)

In this ecstatic vision, Christminster, whose mark is "a halo or glow-fog," seems to send that "message" I mentioned earlier, but it is a message that must be translated from natural to human terms with all the inherent errors of language and its "figures" (part 1, ch. 3). In a moment of revelation, George Eliot's narrator in *Adam Bede* comments that "Nature has her language, and she is not unveracious; but we don't know all the intricacies of her syntax just yet, and in a hasty reading we may happen to extract the very opposite of her real meaning." Now, as Jude attempts to learn the "syntax" of nature's "message," Christminster, through Phillotson, becomes the organizing center of his life: "It had been the yearning of his heart to find something to anchor on, to cling to—for some place which he could call admirable. Should he find that place in this city if he could get there?" (part 1, ch. 3). The phrasing of his question in the rhetorical mode produces a grammatical structure that implies the existence of freedom of choice, when in fact, the pattern of choices has already been established for Jude by his own propensity for misreading. As he answers the questions posed in indirect discourse, beguiled by the transformation his mind has imposed on the scene through figurative language, Jude takes literally his own metaphors of the "new Jerusalem," "the city of light," and "the castle, manned by scholarship and religion" (part 1, ch. 3).

Sue Bridehead is also presented in the metaphoric language that names Christminster. Jude has seen, for example, "the photograph of [her] pretty girlish face, in a broad hat, with radiating folds under the brim like the rays of a halo" (part 2, ch. 1). In fact, the metaphoric process by which Sue will later replace Christminster and Phillotson in Jude's dreams has been facilitated by the nature of Jude's language long before he is even conscious of Sue: earlier, he had become "so romantically attached to Christminster that, like a young lover alluding to his mistress, he felt bashful at mentioning its name" (part 1, ch. 3). The transfer from Phillotson, to Christminster, and finally to Sue as metaphors of that sustaining vision is thus a simple, determined step. Jude's false reading of Sue at a chapel in Christminster as being "ensphered by the same harmonies as those which floated into his ears" leads him to conclude that he has "at last found anchorage for his thoughts" (part 2, ch. 3). When Jude finally meets Sue, he approaches her cautiously and speaks to her as he has spoken of Christminster, "with the bashfulness of a lover" (part 2, ch. 4). At each step in the evolution of his story, his controlling dream is a fiction that he imposes on wayward circumstances.

From the beginning then, the object of desire is not "real" in any sense, but is a "phantasmal" (part 2, ch. 2) creation of Jude's own mind, as are the "ghosts" that haunt Christminster. For Jude, however, the ghosts of his desires disappearing into the "obscure alleys" of Christminster are as real as Arabella's "disappearance into space" (part 2, ch. 1). Constituting himself as a whole subject by an identification with another who repeatedly disappears, "A hungry soul in pursuit of a full soul" (part 3, ch. 10), Jude is accordingly threatened by the possibility of disappearing too: "Jude began to be impressed with the isolation of his own personality, as with a self-spectre . . . seeming thus almost his own ghost" (part 2, ch. 1). Phillotson, Christminster, Arabella, and most strikingly, Sue, thus become the figures of an ideal paradise, which is fundamentally inaccessible, insofar as it is one more metaphor in a structuring system of substitutions and exchanges of phantasmal dreams. The displacement of desire among the various characters points out the existence of a symbolic order, which creates the idea of autonomy when, in fact, the characters exist determined by their propensity for interpretive error.

As an exegetic scholar, "divining rather than beholding the spirit" of his texts (part 1, ch. 5), Jude can never resist the temptation to read deep meanings, the "assemblage of concurring and converging probabilities" of "truths," into a scene (part 2, ch. 1). Yet it is less "absolute certitude" that lies hidden beneath the manifest content of human experience in the novel than it is a mystified, but nonetheless threatening, organization of that content. When Jude thereafter looks into Sue's "untranslatable eyes" (part 2, ch. 2) and immediately begins to interpret her character, he is only repeating the established pattern of error. Despite the difference in the agency that produces it, Jude manifests again the desire for that earlier "law of transmutation." Here, Sue's eyes reveal a text to be translated; but, as with the Greek and Latin grammars, no master code exists to guarantee the authority of Jude's translation. The rules governing the metonymic transfer, the figure Latin rhetoric calls *transmutio,* belong to the same illusion of a metaphysics of presence in the word, and to the same hallucination of a language determined on the basis of a verbal representation. Just as language is constituted through repetition, so too does Jude's life acquire a narratable consistency. But the symbolic "inscription" of Jude's desires upon the surface of Wessex as he travels its roads from Christminster to Shaston, to Aldbrickham and back again, constitutes only the provisional creation of meaning through a process of deferment. As Jude's dreams are transmuted from Arabella to Christminster, and to Sue, the fantasy of stability creates an apparently meaningful and readable text. It is always only in retrospect, however, that Jude's perceptions of those illusions of totality and stability can be organized and lived as an aesthetically coherent *meaning*.

But it is more the inner tensions produced by the characters' shifting relations that shape the action than haphazard or indifferent circumstance. And it is not entirely coincidental that the act of reading surfaces again to indicate these changes in connection with the constant letters that reaffirm the importance of writings, signs, inscription, and marks in the lives of these characters. Altogether there are at least thirty-two letters indicated or implied in the novel, ranging from one-line suicide notes (*"Done because we are too menny"*) to full-sized "carefully considered epistle[s]" (part 6, ch. 4), directly or indirectly narrated, delivered or not delivered. The numerous instances of inscriptions and carvings reinforce the importance of the "letter" in the text as the emblem for the force of illusion.

The first of these letters between Jude and Sue had simply called for their initial meeting, but it was "one of those documents which, simple and commonplace in themselves, are seen retrospectively to have been pregnant with impassioned consequences" (part 2, ch. 4). By the time Sue is engaged to Phillotson, Jude is receiving sudden "passionate" letters (part 3, ch. 1) from her that seem to close the psychic distance between them in a way that they can never quite imitate in person. "'It is very odd—'" Jude says at one point, "'That you are often not so nice in your real presence as you are in your letters!'" "'Does it really seem so to you?'" asks Sue, who then replies, "'Well, that's strange; but I feel just the same about you, Jude'" (part 3, ch. 6). A letter is a medium that effectively separates the writer from the effects of the message, while the message received is often one created by the reader himself. Even in their coldest tones, Sue's letters, while banishing Jude, nevertheless constantly summon him to her by the very fact that they establish a link of communication between them. Similarly, Phillotson's letter relinquishing Sue paradoxically begins reestablishing his hold on her; for the "shadowy third" (part 4, ch. 5), like the substantial couple, is always primarily constituted by this act of communication.

Moreover, when Sue writes a letter, she simultaneously removes and retains her absence and distance. This simultaneity of absence and presence is primarily an outcome of written discourse and is indicative of Jude's more general mystification concerning the existence of a stabilizing meaning. Sue is an eminently desirable woman, but she also becomes a sign in Jude's mind for an absent source of meaning. Accordingly, the act of writing becomes a bolster for the illusion of presence and wholeness within a discourse that appears innocent and transparent. Sue's letter can never replace her, but, conversely, her "real presence" is never identical with the original self promised in the letter. The written word does not allow access to the thing in itself, but always creates a copy, a simulacrum of it that sometimes moves the reader of the word more strongly than can the actual presence of the represented thing. Thus, the curious result is that the graphic sign, rather than the actual presence, of the desired becomes the cause of emotive energy. For Jude, the desire for this originary "anchoring point" becomes an indispensable illusion situated in the syntax of a dream without origin.

The intersubjective complex that structures the novel *Jude the Obscure* offers us some version of the following schema:

1) dreams that fail—Jude, Phillotson, Sue
2) marriages that fail—Jude and Arabella; Sue and Phillotson; Jude and Sue; Arabella and Cartlett; both sets of parents; the legendary ancestor (mentioned in part 5, ch. 4)
3) returns to original failures—Jude and Arabella at Christminster; Sue and Phillotson at Marygreen

We began, remember, with Jude and Arabella at Marygreen, and with Sue and Phillotson at Christminster. The intervening movements in the plot that lead to the present renewal of the characters' former relations thus trace the pattern that characterizes the narrative structure. It is a *chiasmus,* the cross-shaped substitution of properties: the original couples are reunited, but in reverse locales. Hardy had referred to this structure more obliquely as the "geometric construction" behind his novel. Elsewhere he calls it the "quadrille" that puts in motion the opposing qualities of the four main characters. But it turns out that the very process of "construction" that the characters' actions enact is really one more reversal of earlier misguided "constructions." Would it not follow then that this new turn should restore the characters to their "proper" places? That is, if Jude and Sue have been improperly associated at Christminster, might we not recover a measure of truth by simply restoring her to Phillotson at Marygreen? Since this structure of reversal is not only at work on the thematic level of the story, within the marital relationships among the characters, but also animates the greater structure of the narrative, the plot itself, the deconstruction of its pattern has significant implications for the novel's concept of a readable, constructive, integrating process in general.

Jude's idea of a synthetic "anchoring point" of semantic stability originates as the effect of a prior requirement, namely, the requirement that the elements of that synthesis can themselves be permanently fixed in relation to stable qualities. Failing to integrate the ideal and the real with Sue, Jude is no more likely to do so with Arabella. Sue's situation with Phillotson and Jude is even more complex, for the two are versions of the same in different registers. Further reversals, consequently, promise only continued instability. And, I would say, it makes little difference in this novel whether one calls the trope governing the structure of the narrative metaphor, metonymy, chiasmus, or simply a "geometric construction," for from the first, the characters' roles have been inscribed in the determining contextual system defined by the marriage laws.

In the Victorian novel marriage is preeminently the foundation of social stability. As a quasi-contractual agreement, it sets up the participants as a center for other integrating relationships. These relationships are not simply necessary for society; they constitute it. And that larger social and historical life, the world of symbolic relationships, forms in dialectical turn the structure that orders individual behavior in Hardy's novels. In a moment of pure poetic insight Sue comments on the nature of those relations:

> I have been thinking . . . that the social moulds civilization fits us into have no more relation to our actual shapes than the conventional shapes of the constellations have to the real star-patterns. I am called Mrs. Richard Phillotson, living a calm wedded life with my counterpart of that name. But I am not really Mrs. Richard Phillotson, but a woman tossed about, all alone, with aberrant passions, and unaccountable antipathies.
>
> (part 4, ch. 1)

With remarkable clarity Sue recognizes that the social woman is a representation, transposed and supplemented by desire, of her real self. But the relation between her natural and social selves is like the relation between "real star-patterns" and traditional interpretations of the "conventional" constellation shapes, like that between a referent and its linguistic sign—that is, *aesthetic* and hence *arbitrary*. The concept of the self is the product of an aberrant substitution of rhetorical properties. Sue here clearly understands that this rhetorical operation is at best a metaphorical, interpretive act—one that is necessarily open to a variety of figural misreadings.

We have seen that the law that regulates marriage ties in this novel superimposes the kingdom of *culture* on that of *nature*. Following its dictates, Jude artificially imposes a vision of organic totality (figured at different times by Phillotson, Christminster, Sue, etc.) onto nature and accords it a moral and epistemological privilege. In contrast, the narrator's ironic comments show Jude's substitutions and realignments within the marriage system and within the pattern of metaphors for his vision of an "anchoring point" to be purely formal, analogous only by contingency, and hence without privilege. When the value of those associations is questioned, when the notion of Sue as the representation of Jude's dreams is made problematic, the possibility of a simple relation between signified and signifier is also questioned.

That formerly unquestioned assumption is the original moment of illusion that the narrative demystifies. The narrator reveals to us that Jude's and Sue's notion of a privileged system of law is an hypothesis, or a fictional construct (a *doxa*), that makes the orderly conduct of human affairs possible. It is not a "true" and irrefutable axiom based on knowledge (an *episteme*). Their tendency, as revealed by the metaphorical rhetoric of their desires, is always to abide by the lawful order of "natural" logic and unity: "'It is,'" Sue says at one point, "'none of the natural tragedies of love that's love's usual tragedy in civilized life, but a tragedy artificially manufactured for people who in natural state would find relief in parting!'" (part 4, ch. 2). But if the order of "natural" law is itself a hypothetical construct rather than a "natural" occurrence in the world, then there is no necessary reason to suppose that it can, in fact, provide "relief." And it is Sue once again, who, after the tragic deaths of their children, perceives that possibility when she says to Jude:

> "We said . . . that we would make a virtue of joy. I said it was Nature's intention, Nature's law and *raison d'être* that we should be joyful in what instincts she afforded us—instincts which civilization had taken upon itself to thwart. . . . And now Fate has given us this stab in the back for being such fools as to take Nature at her word!"
>
> (part 6, ch. 2)

Jude, who likes to think of himself "as an order-loving man" of an "unbiased nature" (part 4, ch. 2), can only stand by helplessly as he hears Sue destroy the basis of their "natural" marriage.

Hardy's novel situates itself explicitly within the context of the marriage laws that establish Victorian society. It portrays, as Hardy tells us, the attempted translation of the law of nature into civil terms. The characters, however, cannot legitimately perform this translation without confusing the names of two such divergent semantic fields as those covered by "natural law" and "civil law." Confusion arises because the terms designate contextual properties, patterns of integration and disintegration, and not absolute concepts. In Hardy's Wessex, the "law of nature" designates a state of relational integration that precedes in degree the stage of "civil law" since civil law only "enunciates" what is already present in nature to be read. The undoing of a system of relations codified in "civil law" will always reveal, consequently, a more fragmented stage that can be called "natural." This prior stage does not possess moral or epistemological priority over the system that is being undone. But Jude always does assign it priority.

Remembering that "his first aspiration—towards academical proficiency—had been checked by a woman, and that his second aspiration—toward apostleship—had also been checked by a woman," Jude asks himself ungallantly "'Is it . . . that the women are to blame; or is it the artificial system of things, under which the normal sex-impulses are turned into devilish domestic gins and springs to noose and hold back those who want to progress?'" (part 4, ch. 3). The weight of the second clause of the question makes it simply rhetorical: the women are of course not to blame. Although the "natural" pattern that Jude and Sue attempt to substitute for the accepted "civil" one is itself one system of relations among others, they see it as the sole and true order of things and not as an artifice like civil structure. But once the fragmentation of the apparently stable structure of civil law is initiated, endless other versions of "natural law" might be engendered in a repeating pattern of regression.

The decisive term characterizing Jude's and Sue's relationship, "natural law," thus presents itself to be read as a chiastic pattern also. Natural law deconstructs civil law; but natural law is then itself open to the process of its own analysis. Far from denoting a stable point of homogeneity, where they might enact the mythic integration of their "one person split in two" (part 4, ch. 4), the "natural law" of Hardy's Wessex connotes the impossibility of integration and stability. Any of Hardy's texts that put such polarities as natural and civil law, desire and satisfaction, repetition and stability into play will have to set up the fiction of a synthetic process that will function both as the deconstructive instrument and as the outcome of that deconstruction. For Hardy, dualisms are never absolute. Deconstruction, however, is the process that both reveals the deluded basis of the desire for the synthesis of dualism, and also creates the elements necessary for a new and equally deluded desire for integration. *Jude the Obscure* thus both denies the validity of the metaphor that unites "natural" and "civil" law, and elaborates a new metaphor to fulfill the totalizing function of the original binary terms. This new metaphor of life as an organic and orderly process now allows the narrative to continue by providing a myth of a future moment when, as Phillotson's friend Gillingham says, Jude and Sue might make "their union legal . . . and all would be well, and decent, and in order" (part 6, ch. 4). This mythic moment, however, never comes.

It is crucial, then, that the basic conflicts of the novel occur within the "give and take" of marriage, for it situates the issue directly in the referential contexts of ethics and legality. Civil law, in fact, can be conceived as the emblem of referentiality *par excellence* since its purpose is to codify the rules for proper social intercourse. But to abide by the law, we must be able to read its text; ignorance is after all, in English common law, no excuse. Attempting to read it, Jude concludes that "we are acting by the letter; and 'the letter killeth'!" (part 6, ch. 8). Jude thus interprets the Pauline dictum, "The letter killeth but the spirit giveth life," as an injunction against a *literal* reading of the codes governing ethical action. Yet his *figural* reading leads to no spiritual truth either. On the contrary, Jude's illusions result from a figurative language taken literally, as with Sue he takes "Nature at her word." For Jude and Sue, then, there is no text present anywhere that is yet to be transmuted, yet to be translated from natural to civil terms. There is no *natural* truth written anywhere that might be read without being somehow altered in the process. The text of associations Jude fabricates around him is already woven of interpretations and differences in which the meaning of dreams and the desire for illusions are unnaturally coupled. Everything in Wessex "begins" with repetition, with secondary images of a meaning that was never present but whose *signified* presence is reconstituted by the supplementary and belated word of Jude's desires.

I am saying, of course, that the narrative of *Jude the Obscure,* while telling the story of Jude's and Sue's unhappy marriages, also dispels the illusion of a readable truth; that the novel gains its narrative consistency by the repeated undoing of the metaphor of life as organic unity. But the story that tells why figurative denomination is an illusion is itself *readable* and *referential* to the negative truth that Jude never perceives, and the story thus relapses into the very figure it deconstructs. The structure of the narrative as chiasmus, the cross-shaped substitution of properties, also tells, therefore, another story in the form of allegory about the divergence between the literal and figural dimensions of language. That the text reverts to doing what it has claimed to be impossible is not a sign of Hardy's weakness as a novelist, for the error is not with the text, nor with the reader who attempts to understand it. Rather, I would say that with Jude we find that language itself, to the extent that it attempts to be truthful, necessarily misleads us about its own ability to take us outside its own structures in search of meaning.

The myth of a stabilizing nature or civil law, then, is actually the representation of our will to make society seem a unified and understandable organism. But Hardy's novel persists in showing society's laws as open to subversion by the actions of the individuals who make up society. In everyday life, there is an ever possible discontinuity between the word of the law, its spirit, and the practice, the letter, of the law. And the necessary failure of the law to enforce its monologic interpretations of the infinite variety of human behavior can lead to the subversion of the entire relational system. This explains why Jude, by his actions, constantly and unintentionally subverts the Word that he figures in Sue and in his dreams of a university career.

In applying the accepted social law to themselves, Jude and Sue constitute a version of the law, but in applying the general law to their particular situation, they instantaneously alter it. Rather than serving as a source of universal order from which social relations might be stabilized and unified within a social totality, the accepted social law exhibits its inability to constrain the heterogeneity of social relations. The law, then, is always shown to be grammatically structured, since it always engenders only a contingent, contextual meaning. Jude's revolutionary attempt to establish a ground for authentic meaning thus produces an anarchy of mutually exclusive readings of the one piece of language, "The letter killeth." This discontinuity between the "letter" and the "spirit" of the law, between a literal and a figural reading of its sign, is what constitutes Hardy's break with referentiality. Although the law indicates that "The letter killeth," Jude finds it impossible to decide what is the *letter* and what the *spirit* of the law. In each reading, whether within a "natural" or a "civil" system, the law is transposed, altered, and led to produce the conditions for its own undoing. Like Sue's ambiguous letters, the law is consequently only a promise (which cannot be kept) of a future stability and is never adequate to deal with the instability of the present moment.

The repetitions in the novel put at stake not only the relation between Jude's present actions and his family's history, but also the very readability of the initial text of that history. Everywhere about him, history calls out to be read, but Jude consistently fails to do so properly. Because he cannot read it, his actions are never simply a representation of that past, but are an interpretation that has gone awry. Since the novel is itself a kind of history, it too is open to all the errors of interpretation of which it speaks. Hardy's "Postscript," which calls attention to the decisive issues of reading and interpretation, must thus be seen in retrospect as an ironic repetition of the situation dramatized in *Jude* concerning the impossibility of authoritative readings, for it accuses the reader of partaking in Jude's error. We cannot read the novel as Jude reads the motto of his life, that is, with the expectation of encountering an ideally sanctioned stable truth.

But how *are* we to read it then? If the notion of representation is to be at all meaningful, we must presuppose the stability of subjects with stable names who are to be represented, and a rapport between the sign and the referent in the language of the representation. Yet both conditions are absent from this text (notoriously so in the allegorical figure of little Father Time). We can, of course, discern similarities among the characters' various actions. And as we read, attempting, in Hardy's words, "to give shape and coherence to this series of seemings," we too must rely on Jude's example in constructing an interpretive model. But we cannot accept his model of metaphoric synthesis as an absolute. Jude's model of metaphor (governing the patterns of idealization and substitution) is erroneous because it believes in its own referential meaning—it believes that the inwardly desired "anchoring point" can be concretely encountered in the external world as Phillotson, as Christminster, as Arabella, or as Sue. It assumes a world in which literal and figural properties can be isolated, exchanged, and substituted. For the reader and the narrator, metaphoric synthesis persists within the interpretive act, but not as the ground of ultimate reconciliations. Jude himself, however, remains caught in the error of metaphor. But it is an error without which reading could not take place.

We thus find that Hardy's narrative puts the assurance of the truth of the referent into question. But in making this situation thematic, it does allow a meaning, the text, to exist. We are not dealing simply with an *absence* of meaning, for if we were, then that very absence would itself constitute a referent. Instead, as an allegory of the breakdown of the referential system, *Jude the Obscure* continues to refer to its own chiastic operations. This *new* referentiality is one bounded strictly by the margins of textuality. In our courses on the nineteenth-century novel we find it convenient to use *Jude* as a "transitional" text; it is either the last of the Victorians or the first of the Moderns. Morton Zabel has written, for instance, that Hardy was "a realist developing toward allegory . . . who brought the nineteenth century novel out of its slavery to fact." This seems to me fine, as far as it goes. But I would add that this allegorical pattern manifests itself in *Jude* primarily through the subversive power of the dialogic word, which refuses to be reduced to the single "anchoring point" of a transcendent and determining Will, Immanent or otherwise.

As Hardy came to see early on, the function of realistic fiction was to show that *"nothing* is as it appears." It is no wonder, then, that Hardy's last novel was misread. The suggestive and poetic force of *Jude* arises less from its positive attempt to represent appearance than from its rejection of any vision pretending to convey the totality and complexity of life. Accordingly, in *Jude* Hardy repudiates the notion that fiction can ever be Truth, that it can ever "reproduc[e] in its entirety the phantasmagoria of experience with infinite and atomic truth, without shadow, relevancy, or subordination." He dramatizes, instead, the recognition that in narrative "Nothing but the illusion of truth can permanently please, and when the old illusions begin to be penetrated, a more natural magic has to be supplied." To be realistic, the text must proceed as if its representing systems correspond to those in the world; it must create a new illusion of reference to replace the old of representation.

But this transmutation of illusions modifies the original considerably. Like Sue's "real presence," perpetually deviating from the ideal figure of Jude's dreams, the letter of the text, *"translat[ing]* the qualities that are already there" in the world, contains after all only the inadequate ciphers of the spirit of meaning, not the "thing" itself. The deconstruction of the metaphorical model of substitution and translation (operating in Jude's various desires for Christminster, Sue, natural law, etc.) is performed by the rhetorical structure of chiasmus, whose own figural logic both asserts and denies referential authority. From the reader's point of view, the results of each of the figural movements can then be termed "meanings," but only by forgetting that the resulting sociological, ethical, legal, or thematic categories are undone by the very process that creates them.

It may well be, therefore, that Hardy's final novel does not "mean"; but it does signify to a redoubtable degree. It signifies the laws of language over which neither Hardy nor his readers can exercise complete control. To read those laws is to undermine their intent. This is why Hardy, like Jude who adds to the textual allegory of Wessex and generates its history while marking its closure, is bound to allegorical narratives: he creates the fiction of an ideal reader while he constructs a narrative about the illusion of privileged readings. On this level of rhetorical self-consciousness, prose fiction is on the verge of becoming poetry.

"The Spirit Unappeased and Peregrine": *Jude the Obscure*

Philip M. Weinstein

> "It is a city of light," he said to himself.
>
> "The tree of knowledge grows there," he added a few steps further on.
>
> "It is a place that teachers of men spring from and go to."
>
> "It is what you may call a castle, manned by scholarship and religion."
>
> After this figure he was silent a long while, till he added:
>
> "It would just suit me."

Alone and in a setting which fails wholly to corroborate his utterance, Jude sounds a characteristic note of the novel. He would be where he is not, and he has only words to express this desire. More than Hardy's other novels, *Jude the Obscure* stresses the importance and the impotence of words, the huge arena between actuality and ideality which they fill. Jude's Christminster is a place less visualized than conceptualized, a mirage of words—"the tree of knowledge . . . what you may call a castle manned by scholarship and religion." He imagines it as existing spatially "out there" while Hardy reveals it, through Jude's words, as a fabric of "figures," woven from "in here." When Jude resolves, in one transcendent apotheosis, to house his spirit in its ideal home, he ignores the extensive gap between actual and ideal, the instrumental steps necessary if one would try to journey from the one realm to the other. On a scale unique in Hardy's work, this novel insists on

---

From *The Semantics of Desire: Changing Models of Identity from Dickens to Joyce.* © 1984 by Princeton University Press.

the hopelessness of making that journey, and on the fraudulence of its imagined end. The novel spreads before its hero, not the transcendental home of the spirit, but innumerable halfway houses that betray the spirit even as they promise it material abode.

"There was no law of transmutation," Jude learns in his painstaking study of the classical languages. No key exists that will magically ease his transformation from artisan to savant, transposing the languages of learning to the grammar of his native discourse. Between Jude and knowledge there lie the certainty of years of study, the risk of faulty pedagogic methods, the obstacle of immovable class prejudice. Jude remains childlike in his approach to these barriers. Seeking unconditional union with the ideal itself, he hardly hesitates over the means for this achievement:

> What was most required by citizens? Food, clothing, and shelter. An income from any work in preparing the first would be too meagre; for making the second he felt a distaste; the preparation of the third requisite he inclined to. They built in a city; therefore he would learn to build.

In his mind's eye he is already there. His clichés as to a profession have no specific reference. The actual conditions of his approach, like the actual conditions of Christminster, are scarcely considered. Jude moves absentmindedly through the material of his life—its contingent days and places—enamored of the immaterial absolute, bruising himself on the fleshed-out conditional. He seeks, outside himself, a perfect receptacle for his immaculate spirit. He finds, outside himself, no such receptacle but instead a bewildering array of strictly human approximations: not pure but adulterate, not ideal but embodied, not transcendentally given but mediated and ambiguous. The landscape of *Jude the Obscure,* unlike that of *Tess of the D'Urbervilles,* is overwhelmingly cultural. The landmarks within it comprise the range of human institutions and conventions by which the journeying spirit finds itself stymied rather than fulfilled: a landscape of signifiers emptied of those meanings they promise. If the basic unit of *Tess* is the blood, the basic unit of *Jude* is the word. (In *Jude* wounds are expressed through talk, not blood.) If the world of *Tess* is mainly the horizontal one of natural immersion, the world of *Jude* is the vertical one of cultural aspiration, counterfeit, and failure.

Jude is Hardy's most insistent seeker—his characteristic posture is dedication—and he inhabits a novel crammed with advertisement, with signifying artifacts that promise to fulfill the seeker's desire, to connect him with his goal. At the simplest level of false advertisement there are Arabella's dimple and false hair, Vilbert's quack medicine, the adulterated beer whose impurities Arabella (but not Jude) detects. At the next level, not deceptive in themselves but slippery in their relation to the seeker, are the icons of Greek and biblical culture—the statues of Venus and Apollo, the Latin cross and the Ten Commandments—which misleadingly propose a realizable harmony between acolyte and symbolized values. (The most pathetic instances of icons that express the gap, rather than connection, between worshipper and sacred image are the models— first of wood and then of cake—that Jude constructs of Christminster.) More diffuse are the secular institutions of education and profession, of marriage and divorce. Designed to bestow communal structure and purpose upon inchoate human desire, these institutions remain oblique to the movement of Jude's and Sue's actual lives. In their role as the culture's licensed forms for individual thought and feeling, they act as false beacons, beyond following, beyond ignoring. As Robert Heilman suggests, they are inextricably woven into the fabric of the characters' consciousness.

Misleading connectives, promising to deliver the spirit of its burden or connect it with its goal, punctuate the novel. Jude and Sue tirelessly write each other letters, seeking to express their deep selves and to make contact with the other. The letters are more eloquent than speech. By ignoring the disconcerting presence of an interlocutor, they succeed, if not in telling the truth, at least in making a narrative of their lives.

The fundamental category of a misleading mediator, a connective that fails to make good on its promise, is language itself. *Jude the Obscure* uses discourse in a thoroughly modern way, unique in Hardy's novels; the words a character uses appear less as the transparent bearer of private spirit than as the opaque, already motivated property of a public culture: the words have already been coopted. (Words as the property of an alien culture engage Conrad and Joyce massively, and I return to this theme in my discussion of these later writers [elsewhere].) What may be most obscure about Jude Fawley and Sue Bridehead is that, at the center of their being, they are mute. The language they have access to—and it pours out of them helplessly, it is the blood of their spirit—is often an incoherent amalgam of the commonplaces of their culture, more faithful to the psychic stresses of a Swinburne or Newman, a J. S. Mill or Matthew Arnold (whom they are echoing) than to their own inarticulable need.

A. Alvarez is right when he claims that "the essential subject of the novel is not Oxford, or marriage, or even frustration. It is loneliness." Jude and Sue's abundant speech only accentuates their separateness. Alvarez (and J. I. M. Stewart makes the same point) notes that "no character ever properly seems to connect with another in talk," but this aspect of the novel—which is endemic in Hardy's art—seems to me not a flaw in *Jude the Obscure*. For once Hardy has constructed a novel which accommodates the awkward silence at the core of his vision. The characters are there, given in their completeness, before they are empowered with speech. Speech is, as it were, a late accomplishment of the species, more capable of releasing chorus-like platitudes than of articulating individual need. The spoken words proliferate in *Jude the Obscure* like cartoon utterances, cascading like soap-bubbles from the already finished figures who remain mute beside their utterance.

Whether such effects of verbal alienation are intentional or not, the novel certainly renders the conditional thinness, the ardent abstractedness of Jude's dedication to western culture. He has its words, but they never sound quite like his own. J. I. M. Stewart writes:

> We are nowhere made to *feel* what brought him his Greek
> and Latin; he is seen in virtually no concrete situation relevant
> to it. . . . Again, the extended passage in which Jude is rep-
> resented as wandering about Christminster and hearing the
> ghostly *ipsissima verba* of departed Oxford men . . . is a poor
> and even embarrassing substitute for something not really
> created in the book.

"No concrete situation . . . something not really created": that is less the novel's problem than its elusive achievement. Indeed, it is not surprising that this facet of Hardy's art should be more pronounced in *Jude the Obscure* than in his other novels. Only here is the protagonists' discourse insistently intellectual; elsewhere they do not proclaim their insertion within this or that larger cultural tradition. Insofar as the insertion is itself suspect—revealing the protagonists' isolation rather than their belonging—then the abstractness of the urged positions, the precarious purchase of the speaker upon his own utterance, is itself germane. Jude's relation to his sought-after culture *is* ghostly and abstract rather than fleshed-out and instrumental; it is right that he should enter the city at night, hearing its medley of disembodied voices. Jude's great moments at Christminster are equally verbal—his two orations rehearsing "the Articles of his Belief, in the Latin tongue" and grappling with the "difficult question" of his intellectual career—and on these occasions Hardy stresses the only facet of Christminster available to Jude: its words.

Jude is so enamored of these words that he tends to speak them as a substitute for his own, and even the "autobiographical" sketch he gives of himself in that last oration is ringed round with ironies. It is a speech "from the heart" delivered to a coarse and unreceptive audience rather than to the university hearers he craves, and it is not the truth of Jude but the "story" of Jude, the fiction he must shape to deliver himself at all:

> It takes two or three generations to do what I tried to do in one; and my impulses—affections—vices perhaps they should be called—were too strong not to hamper a man without advantages. . . . I was, perhaps, after all, a paltry victim to the spirit of mental and social restlessness, that makes so many unhappy in these days! . . . And what I appear, a sick and poor man, is not the worst of me. I am in a chaos of principles—groping in the dark—acting by instinct and not after example.

In each of its twists (the speech begins on a cheerful note but turns bitter and self-indicting as it goes on), Jude's oration exaggerates and distorts his nature. Successively presenting himself as too impatient, too impulsive, too passionate, too restless, in "a chaos of principles," Jude's words miss the naïve sweetness and hesitancy, the gently yearning idealism, the desire to respond coupled with the baffled resentment of failure, that most deeply characterize his way of encountering experience. (Some such rationale is needed to place a passage like the following:

> "You know what a weak fellow I am. My two Arch Enemies you know—my weakness for womankind and my impulse to strong liquor. Don't abandon me to them, Sue, to save your own soul only! They have been kept entirely at a distance since you became my guardian-angel!"

This is plausibly how Jude would characterize himself but certainly not— in its capitalized simplicities—an accurate portrait. Eliot's Sweeney says, "I gotta use words when I talk to you," and Jude's words are likewise condemned to come from a cultural stockpile and therefore to remain at a distance from the private dilemma they would describe. Though he pursues a different argument, Jerome H. Buckley also notes the inaccuracy of Jude's self-portrait: "Jude is neither the drunkard nor the amorist; he is betrayed by ordinary appetites and feelings, by his own temperament, and perhaps most of all by the disparity between flesh and spirit in the world itself, the distance between the real and the ideal.") Jude is no Prometheus, no peer of Huxley or Spencer; nor is he an impulsive man, raging in the dark. Rather, he is a mild and civil man, confused by the words and promises of others and by the flux of possibilities within himself, a man who really seeks, in Lawrence's fine phrase, "not a store of learning, nor the vanity of education . . . [but] to find conscious expression for that which he held in his blood" ("The Study of Thomas Hardy"). Had he discovered that the richness he yearned for lay inchoate in his own blood, he might have succeeded in forging an authentic voice.

As it is, both Jude and Sue rely upon one external voice after another to make sense of their confusing experience. At their nadir, Father Time's murder of himself and the two younger children, they engage in a desperate game of quotations, seeking to alleviate their misery by finding a previously articulated ground for what would otherwise seem unbearably groundless:

> "No," said Jude. "It was in his nature to do it. The doctor says there are such boys springing up amongst us. . . ."
>
> She sobbed again. "O, O my babies! They had done no harm! Why should they have been taken away, and not I!"
>
> There was another stillness—broken at last by two persons in conversation somewhere without.
>
> "They are talking about us, no doubt!" moaned Sue. "'We are made a spectacle unto the world, and to angels, and to men!' . . . There is something external to us which says, 'You shan't!' First it said, 'You shan't learn!' Then it said, 'You shan't labour!' Now it says, 'You shan't love!' . . . I talked to the child as one should only talk to people of mature age. I said the world was against us, that it was better to be out of life than in it at this price; and he took it literally. . . . We went about loving each other too much—indulging ourselves to utter selfishness with each other! We said—do you remember?—that we would make a virtue of joy. I said it was Nature's intention . . . It is best, perhaps, that they should be gone. . . ."
>
> "Yes," replied Jude. "Some say that the elders should rejoice when their children die in infancy."

"But they don't know!" . . . I am driven out of my mind by things! What ought to be done!" She stared at Jude, and tightly held his hand.

"Nothing can be done," he replied. "Things are as they are, and will be brought to their destined issue."

She paused. "Yes! Who said that?" she asked heavily.

"It comes in the chorus of the *Agamemnon*. It has been in my mind continually since this happened."

These three pages allude to a veritable chorus of voices. Jude and Sue inhabit a world of verbal echoes; they automatically refer the inexplicable events of their lives to the swarm of formulae cluttering their heads. Sue's consciousness is like a larder stocked with nothing but phrases. She has so persuaded herself that the key to the children's disaster lies in something she said or failed to say that she (and Jude with her) misses one of the primary causes silently visible to every reader: the paucity of wordless physical affection has scarred Father Time as deeply as any utterance. It is typical of Sue and Jude to overlook such an incarnate cause, as they despairingly cast about among their treasury of remembered sayings for an intellectual formulation that will fit the case. None does fit the case, and at a certain point the accumulation of allusions takes on a tinge of absurdity. The event is so overexplained as to become unexplained. The pointed weight of allusive wisdom suddenly turns arbitrary and weightless—a bandying of words.

It takes the insight of someone like Nietzsche (a thinker whom Hardy cursorily repudiated) to identify the verbal malaise here. Jude and Sue have not impressed upon their discourse the form of their own embodied spirit. They have not mastered the words they utter, making them their own, for Jude and Sue remain trapped within a linguistic world-view which holds that truth is external, universally applicable, and has already been uttered. The purpose of education in such a world-view—and this is the education that Jude seeks—is to acquaint the student with this already articulated body of truths. Nietzsche knows, by contrast, that what passes for a culture's truths are its willed assertions, its claims rather than its discoveries:

Whatever exists, having somehow come into being, is again and again reinterpreted to new ends, taken over, transformed and redirected by some power superior to it; all events in the organic world are a subduing, a *becoming master*, and all subduing and becoming master involves a fresh interpretation, an adaptation through which any previous "meaning" and "purpose" are necessarily obscured or even obliterated.

(On the Genealogy of Morals)

It may now be possible to identify one of the peculiar tensions in *Jude the Obscure.* It is the tension between the morally elusive facts of embodied life, as Hardy presents them, and the static assumptions of discourse, as Sue and Jude reveal them. On the one hand—in the realm of behavior—we find the ever-changing, morally opaque play of power and penetration; and on the other—in the realm of discourse—we find the naïve expectation of a fully appropriate moral paradigm, one that accounts for all contingencies, as promised by the formulae of the Greek and Judeo-Christian traditions. This tension exists in one form or another throughout Hardy's novels, for his vision of behavior is far more sophisticated than his or his protagonists' assumptions about the ways in which their culture's discourse organizes and evaluates experience.

Another way of putting it is to say that Hardy sees the dynamics of behavior with a moral flexibility approaching Nietzschean candor, but that—unlike Nietzsche—he has not extended his perception of life as an interplay of powers into a perception of language as an interplay of powers as well. He stops short of Nietzsche's claim that discourse is not the transparent reflection of a pre-existent and static reality waiting to be named by the words, but rather the mediated expression of a thrusting will to make sense of experience. Discourse is actually as non-transcendental, as unsanctioned and contingent, as the experience that it is meant to organize: a dilemma that Hardy seems more to reveal than to acknowledge. Put most simply, since all discourse is inflected by will, Jude and Sue will either inflect their terms so as to express their own experience or parrot the terms that express someone else's experience. Thus, to return to Nietzsche's verb, Jude and Sue do not *master* the meaning of Father Time's act because they do not personally will that knowledge into consciousness and language with sufficient intensity. Borrowers rather than makers of discourse, they do not generate, from their own anguish, the native phrasing that will put them in touch with their own inchoate experience. Their dependence on prefabricated formulae marks their evasion of (to paraphrase Lawrence) that which they hold unseeing in their own blood. Through borrowed discourse they remain obscure to their own necessities, looking passively without for explanations that lie unformulated within. As Howells remarked in 1895, "All the characters, indeed, have the appealing quality of human beings really doing what they must while seeming to do what they will."

"What they must" do is dramatized by Hardy, if not conceptualized by Jude and Sue. Arabella's effect upon Jude rarely extends as far upward as his consciousness. He receives "a dumb announcement of affinity *in posse*," and he responds instinctively, "in commonplace obedience to conjunctive orders from headquarters, unconsciously received." "In short, as if materially, a compelling arm of extraordinary muscular power seized hold of him—something which had nothing in common with the spirits and influences that had moved him hitherto." This "muscular power" of Arabella is as unquestionable as it is unexplained, and Hardy shows us how her unwelcome suasion affects Jude's speech even as it bypasses his consciousness. He is not the man openly to air resentment against her (or against anyone), so it must emerge in the disowned duplicity of his language:

> "Of course I never dreamt six months ago, or even three, of marrying. It is a complete smashing up of my plans—I mean my plans before I knew you, my dear. But what are they, after all! Dreams about books, and degrees, and impossible fellowships, and all that. Certainly we'll marry: we must!"

> "Do be quiet, Arabella, and have a little pity on the creature!"
> "Hold up the pail to catch the blood, and don't talk" . . .
> "It is a hateful business!" said he.
> "Pigs must be killed." . . .
> "Thank God!" Jude said. "He's dead."
> "What's God got to do with such a messy job as a pig-killing, I should like to know!" she said scornfully. "Poor folks must live."
> "I know, I know," said he. "I don't scold you."

There is something amiss—literally, something missing—in these speeches, as though Jude's consciousness could not tolerate the tension in his feelings. "I mean my plans before I knew you, my dear" is a feeble lie to Arabella and to himself, and "I don't scold you" is the age-old formulation used to avoid acknowledgment of scolding. Jude is avoiding his own emotional confusions; his language achieves clarity at the expense of candor. Nietzsche refers to this behavior as a particular species of lying: "wishing *not* to see something that one does see; wishing not to see something *as* one sees it. . . . The most common lie is that with which one lies to oneself" (*Twilight of the Idols*).

Jude's discourse with Sue displays as well these pockets of disin-
genuousness:

> "Of course I may have exaggerated your happiness—one
> never knows," he continued blandly.
>
> "Don't think that, Jude, for a moment, even though you
> may have said it to sting me! . . . If you think I am not happy
> because he's too old for me, you are wrong."
>
> "I don't think anything against him—to you, dear."

When he takes her hand a little later, she draws it away. He then retorts
that his gesture is innocent and cousinly, whereupon she repents but
insists on apprising Phillotson that he has held it:

> "O—of course, if you think it necessary. But as it means
> nothing it may be bothering him needlessly."
>
> "Well—are you sure you mean it only as my cousin?"
>
> "Absolutely sure. I have no feelings of love left in me."
>
> "That's news. How has it come to be?"
>
> "I've seen Arabella."
>
> She winced at the hit; then said curiously, "When did you
> see her?"
>
> "When I was at Christminster."
>
> "So she's come back; and you never told me! I suppose you
> will live with her now?"
>
> "Of course—just as you live with your husband."

She winced at the hit: Hardy underlines the strategic skirmishing
within their intimacy. The point is not that Jude is sinister but that he
maintains his obscurity; he will not acknowledge the cutting edge of his
own voice. These two lovers like to speak of their love as something too
sublime for earth, but there is considerable malice lurking in their discourse, and the scene in which he coerces her to marry him by using
the threat of a return to Arabella can only be called extortion. Jude's
behavior . . . is steeped in the exigencies of his embodied feelings, but
his language reflects those exigencies only on condition that it need not
acknowledge them. If this be true of Jude, so much the more does it
apply to Sue.

I shall say little about Sue since she has already received exhaustive
critical commentary. She bears on my argument, however, because it is
through her portrayal that Hardy most asserts and then undermines the
reader's confidence in a common standard of values capable of articu-

lation. "The 'freedom' she has been at such pains to assert," Ian Gregor notes, "and which . . . would seem to have provided an unequivocal point of vantage . . . [begins to be] seen as something much more ambivalent, a nervous self-enclosure, the swift conceptualizing, safeguarding the self against the invasions of experience. Sue's scrutiny is keen, but it is judiciously angled." Sue's verbal assertions are gradually revealed as fully vulnerable to the contortions of her instinctual life. She is uncontrollably capricious, addicted to a coquetry that (in Robert Heilman's words) "is, in the end, the external drama of inner divisions, of divergent impulses each of which is strong enough to determine action at any time, but not at all times or even with any regularity." She is incurably at war with her own body, and her final behavior amply bears out Freud's contention that the sting of conscience is fueled by aggression turned inward. (Freud's fullest discussion of conscience [in *Civilisation and Its Discontents*] provides an unimprovable gloss on Sue Bridehead:

> His [the individual's] aggressiveness is introjected, internalized; it is, in point of fact, sent back to where it came from— that is, it is directed towards his own ego. There it is taken over by a portion of the ego, which sets itself over against the rest of the ego as super-ego, and which now, in the form of "conscience," is ready to put into action against the ego the same harsh aggressiveness that the ego would have liked to satisfy upon other, extraneous individuals. The tension between the harsh super-ego and the ego that is subjected to it, is called by us the sense of guilt; it expresses itself as a need for punishment. . . . As long as things go well with a man, his conscience is lenient and lets the ego do all sorts of things; but when misfortune befalls him, he searches his soul, acknowledges his sinfulness, heightens the demands of his conscience, imposes abstinences on himself and punishes himself with penances.)

Hardy reveals in Sue perhaps his most audacious perceptions about the human aspiration for clarity of purpose and a life devoted to realizing the spirit within. Hardy shows not only that her asserted values have no transcendental basis (they are stained and mediated by the very fact of her being embodied), he shows her bodily grounding to be—itself as well—something opaque and indeterminate, a source of further confusion rather than clarifying authority. She confesses to Jude that "I am called Mrs Richard Phillotson, living a calm wedded life with my counterpart of that name. But I am not really Mrs Richard Phillotson, but a woman tossed about, all alone, with aberrant passions, and unaccountable antipathies." Not really Mrs Richard Phillotson, and not in any clarifying way a woman at all. Jude's great-aunt's friend notes the elusiveness of Sue's natural identity: "She was not exactly a tomboy, you know; but she could do things that only boys do, as a rule."

By way of contrast with such elusiveness, the profound solidity of *Tess of the D'Urbervilles* derives from its hold on sexual identity as something absolute. Sexual identity appears there as an ultimate ground of amoral meaning, lying beneath the relative and collapsible ones of moral assertion. The world of *Jude the Obscure* has become unmoored from this natural certitude. In the portrait of Sue Bridehead Hardy suggests that, to the unappeased spirit in search of articulate paradigms, nothing—not even the body's native stresses—can be reliably categorized. Life is a something foreign to the classificatory demands made by the spirit. In its utterances, its values, and even its bodily grounding, life is a phenomenon of stain, illogic, and obscurity.

Within this context Arabella and Father Time come into focus as the polar opposites of the novel. Arabella lives in the contingent. She is as canny about daily survival and as ignorant of ultimate purposes as Jude is learned in cosmic platitudes and inept in local procedures. She has no goal but knows unerringly the way. She measures accurately the appropriate method for killing a pig just as, during Jude's final illness, she "critically gauge[s] his ebbing life." The stains and deformations of time are unthinkingly accepted by Arabella. Pious and pagan utterances flow forth from her, with equal appositeness, either genuinely attuned to her desire or asserted with conscious hypocrisy. She is true to herself because she recognizes no standard beyond her embodied nature that she could betray. In her very fickleness she places and measures the obscure deceits of others, their attempt to square their incarnate existence with those immaculate values to which it is alien. She is exactly as well adjusted to the meaningless conditions of life as Father Time is incapable of coping with them.

That solemn child is the ultimate doomed Platonist in Hardy's world. Absorbing somewhere in his consciousness the full ravage wrought by time upon value, he has frozen his perception of the world into a posture of unforgivable stasis. He lives in a perpetuated, last-judgment landscape, all things appearing to him in their form of final exhaustion. Accepting time's ravage, he repudiates utterly the mercy and promise of its moment-by-moment process. On the train he passively regards "his companions as if he saw their whole rounded lives rather than their immediate figures." Unlike his mother, whose rough humanity resides in her openness toward process rather than meaning, Father Time has fixed upon an absurd meaning at the expense of process. He "seemed to have begun with the generals of life, and never to have concerned himself with the particulars." His optic can only envisage life as a gathered and complete insult inflicted on himself and others. He is an extreme instance of that mentality that Nietzsche calls "Socratism":

> Wherever Socratism turns its searching eyes it sees lack of insight and the power of illusion; and from this lack it infers the essential perversity and reprehensibility of what exists. Basing himself on this point, Socrates conceives it to be his duty to correct existence.
>
> *(The Birth of Tragedy)*

Father Time corrects existence too. He cancels his role within it.

I began by noting Jude's characteristic desire to be where he is not, a desire that reflects, according to J. Hillis Miller, "the experience of an 'emotional void' within, a distance of oneself from oneself." Miller claims that this absence in Hardy's characters is at last recognized as inalterable, and that they end by seeking the only release conceivable, that of death. More important to my reading of Hardy is the impact of an "emotional void" upon behavior itself: the pockets of dream-like passivity, of mental absence, that lie submerged within his protagonists' most earnest aspirations, waiting to wreck them. Jude and Clym are only the most reflective instances of a range of characters—Troy, Wildeve, Fitzpiers, Henchard among them—whose project, whatever energetic flourish it may begin with, contains a debilitating emptiness within. Their projects fail because all projects, once embarked on, either fail to meet the conditions of daily life or—meeting them—produce ennui and then disabling fatigue. These characters have sufficient energy to scorn the available, not to create alternatives; and this is so, one finally gathers, because their imagination is stocked with nothing but unrealities. The desirable is keyed to a mental vocabulary that simply negates whatever in Hardy's world can be actually experienced. Thus Hardy dramatizes characters whose consciousness of what they want and why they want it remains continuously out of phase with the vagaries of their incarnate behavior. They have no terms for finding out what they are actually doing, and no way of actually doing what they want. Indeed, they seem, in some central part of their being, to be spirits stunned to find themselves placed on earth and embodied in flesh. This gap between the consciousness of essential being and the opacity of contingent existence they express through a lurking and inexpungeable passivity. At critical moments they blank out.

Jude, for example, first slides back into his married routine with Arabella with an eery complicity. She tells him she can get a day off; he finds the notion "particularly uncongenial," yet says, "Of course, if you'd like to, you can." She tells him the train they can take, and he responds, "As you like." She gathers her luggage, "and they went on to the railway, and made the half-hour's journey to Aldbrickham, where they entered a third-rate inn near the station in time for a late supper." They pass the night together. Where, one wants to know, is Jude during this transaction? Bodily, of course, with Arabella, and the effortless complicity of his physical behavior seems dependent on a corresponding mental absence. Jude's spirit has, for the moment, slipped out. Hardy provides no notation of a conflicted state of mind.

Such "absences" mark Jude's spiritual career as well. His campaign displays such a blundering and absentminded sense of purpose that no reader can be surprised by its failure. When, for instance, a casual acquaintance at Marygreen avers that "Such places [as Christminster] be not for such as you," Jude's long-sustained undertaking immediately falters:

> It was decidedly necessary to consider facts a little more closely than he had done of late. . . . "I ought to have thought of this before," he said, as he journeyed back. "It would have been better never to have embarked in the scheme at all than to do it without seeing clearly where I am going, or what I am aiming at."

(Hardy's use of plot is at moments like this so overtly clumsy that one wonders if he is not verging upon intentional absurdity—an intentional repudiation of the salient lines of a strong plot. For instance, when Jude attempts to commit suicide and the ice ignobly refuses to permit his romantic gesture, we are not far from Beckett's impotent Molloy, helplessly setting about, when he has a spare moment, to open his veins, and never succeeding.) Again, one wonders, where has his consciousness been during these previous years of "preparation"? Why is he so unaware of himself as a conditional creature? When under stress he is incapable of looking about him and charting the most intelligent course; instead he leaps into the transcendent and allusive ideal. Consider his behavior when being pressed to remarry Arabella:

> "I don't remember it," said Jude doggedly. "There's only one woman—but I won't mention her in this Capharnaum!"
>
> Arabella looked towards her father. "Now, Mr. Fawley, be honourable," said Donn. "You and my daughter have been living here together these three or four days, quite on the understanding that you were going to marry her. . . . As a point of honour you must do it now."
>
> "Don't say anything against my honour!" enjoined Jude hotly, standing up. "I'd marry the W— of Babylon, rather than do anything dishonourable! No reflection on you, my dear. It is a mere rhetorical figure—what they call in the books, hyperbole."
>
> "Keep your figures for your debts to friends who shelter you," said Donn.
>
> "If I am bound in honour to marry her—as I suppose I am—though how I came to be here with her I know no more than a dead man—marry her I will, so help me God! I have never behaved dishonourably to a woman or to any living thing. I am not a man who wants to save himself at the expense of the weaker among us!"
>
> "There—never mind him, deary," said she, putting her cheek against Jude's. "Come up and wash your face, and just put yourself tidy, and off we'll go. Make it up with father."

The scene is remarkable, and Hardy has no other novel in which one can imagine it. We see strikingly how Jude's allusive words create his "absence" from his coming fate. His mind rises into the empyrean, with Capharnaum, the Whore of Babylon, rhetorical figures, the theme of honor; it will not register the meaning of the specific act he is about to commit. Indeed, he *would* marry the Whore of Babylon because, somehow, his sense of himself remains idealized—permanently astray from, immune to, the sordid physical situations in which he finds himself. One hears a sense of verbally engendered immunity in his bland twaddle about "mere rhetorical figures," and Hardy nicely places Jude's tone of smug caprice, by having Donn retort: "Keep your figures for your debts. . . ." Donn and his daughter are content to humor Jude's proliferation of weightless abstract identities ("I have never . . . I am not . . ."). The more he breezily defines his unfettered spirit, the more easily they exploit his befuddled and conditional body.

What we see in such behavior is absence, and absence increasingly marks Jude's career. (The treatment of Jude and Sue's children, unnamed and of no importance while alive, obsessively and injuriously mourned when dead, reveals the same theme of absence.) He defines himself at first by what he will do, at last by what he has not done. He cherishes at first expectations of what is to be, at last memories of what has not happened. His return to Christminster indicates a final surrender of his attempt—at best half-hearted—to realize himself, to make an authentic home for his unsponsored and unreleased spirit. Thereafter he is given over to the "Remembrance Games." He lives wholly, now, in the schizoid space between failed expectation and ignored actuality, his mind focused on poignant scenarios (more fictive than true) with Sue and Christminster, his body abandoned to approaching death. His last gesture is characteristically verbal—he dies in words—and as usual he is quoting someone else. I think it is crucial to see that he is not Job; he is not an innocent and successful man, massively undone by an unholy pact between God and the devil. Rather, he is obscurely complicit in his own downfall, though it be his peculiar fate never to identify that complicity, never to find the words that will tell him who he is in all his incarnate perplexity. His death scene only gains poignance through its verbal indeterminacy, and it is the apex of Hardy's art that, four pages later, he can create a dialogue between Arabella and the Widow Edlin that matches Jude's death speech in resonance:

> "Did he forgive her!"
> "Not as I know."
> "Well—poor little thing, 'tis to be believed she's found forgiveness somewhere! She said she had found peace!"
> "She may swear that on her knees to the holy cross upon her necklace till she's hoarse, but it won't be true!" said Arabella. "She's never found peace since she left his arms, and never will again till she's as he is now!"

Words at their best reveal the inadequacy of other words, and Hardy puts this last speech with unchallengeable authority in the mouth of Arabella. Rooted in the earth and stained in every way by it, strengthened as much as stained, Arabella places Sue's verbal and emotional evasions before us. Beyond this, though, Arabella's words bear the mark of subjective limitation that is the fate of words in this novel. Behind the verbalized truth that "she's never found peace since she left his arms," there lies, in the silence created by her speech, a truth that is darker yet: that, condemned to a body whose stresses she could neither disown nor make her own, Sue Bridehead found no peace in Jude's arms either. She found no peace anywhere. In this most unsettling of Hardy's novels the obscure spirit is compelled to move, in Eliot's words, "unappeased and peregrine," able to achieve nowhere—not in thought or feeling, not in the discourse of culture or the ground of nature—a form for its embodiment.

Chronology

1840	Thomas Hardy born on June 2 in Higher Bockhampton, a community in the parish of Stinsford, Dorset, the son of Thomas Hardy, a stonemason, and Jemima Hand Hardy.
1848	Begins his education at a school in Lower Bockhampton.
1849	Hardy is moved to a school in Dorchester.
1855	Begins teaching at the Stinsford Church Sunday School.
1856	Hardy is accepted at the office of architect John Hicks as a pupil. Also in this year Hardy meets Horace Moule and William Barnes.
ca. 1860	Hardy writes his first poem, called "Domicilium."
1862	After settling in London, Hardy goes to work for architect and church restorer Arthur Blomfield. He reads widely, studies paintings at the National Gallery, and becomes an agnostic.
1863	The Royal Institute of British Architects awards Hardy an essay prize.
1865	*Chambers' Journal* publishes "How I Built Myself a House." Hardy attends French classes at King's College, Cambridge.
1867	Hardy returns to Dorset and resumes working for John Hicks. At this time he also begins work on his first novel, *The Poor Man and the Lady.*
1868	*The Poor Man and the Lady* is rejected by Macmillan; Hardy resubmits the manuscript to Chapman & Hall.
1869	Hardy meets George Meredith. Begins his second novel, *Desperate Remedies.*
1870	Hardy travels to Cornwall, where he meets Emma Lavinia Gifford, his future wife. Publisher William Tinsley agrees to produce *Desperate Remedies* at the author's expense.

1871   *Desperate Remedies* published. Also in this year Hardy writes *Under the Greenwood Tree* and begins *A Pair of Blue Eyes.*

1872   *Under the Greenwood Tree* published. *A Pair of Blue Eyes* appears in serial form.

1873   Hardy's friend Horace Moule commits suicide. Hardy is invited by Leslie Stephen to contribute to *Cornhill;* Hardy then begins the serialized version of *Far from the Madding Crowd. A Pair of Blue Eyes* is published.

1874   *Far from the Madding Crowd* is published. Hardy marries Emma Lavinia Gifford; they travel to France after the wedding, and upon return settle in Surbiton.

1876   *The Hand of Ethelberta* appears. Hardy and his wife travel to Holland and Germany, and then move to a home at Sturminster Newton, in Dorset.

1878   *The Return of the Native* published. Hardy moves once again, to London, where he is elected to the Savile Club.

1879   Hardy pursues research for *The Trumpet-Major* in the British Museum.

1880   *The Trumpet-Major* published. Hardy meets the Poet Laureate, Alfred, Lord Tennyson. The writing of *A Laodicean* is slowed by a serious illness.

1881   *A Laodicean* published.

1882   *Two on a Tower* published.

1883   Hardy moves to Dorchester where he begins building his home, Max Gate. "The Dorsetshire Labourer" appears in *Longman's Magazine.*

1884   Hardy begins composition of *The Mayor of Casterbridge.*

1885   Moves into Max Gate. Starts writing *The Woodlanders.*

1886   *The Mayor of Casterbridge* published.

1887   *The Woodlanders* published. Hardy visits Italy.

1888   *The Wessex Tales,* a collection of short stories, published. Composition of *Tess of the D'Urbervilles* begins.

1889   Several publishers reject the first installments of *Tess.*

1890   Hardy finishes *Tess.*

1891   Both *Tess of the D'Urbervilles* and *A Group of Noble Dames* are published.

1892   Hardy's father dies. The first version of *The Well-Beloved* is serialized. Relations with his wife begin to deteriorate, and worsen over the next two years, particularly during the composition of *Jude the Obscure.*

1893   Hardy travels to Dublin and Oxford, where he visits Florence Henniker, with whom he writes a short story, and, it is believed, falls in love.

1894   *Life's Little Ironies,* a collection of poems, is published.

1895   *Jude the Obscure* is published and receives primarily outraged reviews. As a result Hardy decides to discontinue novel-writing and henceforward produces only poetry. Also in this year Hardy works on the Uniform Edition of his novels.

1897   *The Well-Beloved* published.

1898   *The Wessex Poems* published.

1901   *Poems of the Past and the Present* published.

1904   *The Dynasts,* part 1 published. Hardy's mother dies.

1905   Hardy receives an Honorary LL.D. from Aberdeen.

1906   *The Dynasts,* part 2 published.

1908   *The Dynasts,* part 3 published.

1909   *Time's Laughingstocks* published. Hardy becomes the governor of the Dorchester Grammar School.

1910   Hardy is awarded the O.M. (Order of Merit).

1912   Hardy's wife Emma Lavinia dies on November 27.

1913   *A Changed Man* is published. Hardy receives an Honorary D.Litt. degree from Cambridge; he is also made an honorary Fellow of Magdalen College, Cambridge.

1914   Hardy marries Florence Emily Dugdale. The collection of poems called *Satires of Circumstance* is published. As World War I begins Hardy joins a group of writers dedicated to the support of the Allied cause.

1915   Hardy's sister Mary dies.

1917   *Moments of Vision,* a collection of poetry, is published.

1919   Hardy's first *Collected Poems* is published.

1920   Oxford University awards Hardy an Honorary D.Litt.

1921   *Late Lyrics and Earlier* published. Hardy becomes honorary Fellow at Queen's College, Oxford.

1923   *The Famous Tragedy of the Queen of Cornwall* published. Hardy receives a visit from the Prince of Wales at Max Gate.

1925   *Human Shows* is published.

1928   Hardy dies on January 11; his ashes are buried at Westminster Abbey, and his heart is placed at his first wife's grave in the Stinsford churchyard. *Winter Words* published posthumously. Florence Emily Hardy publishes *The Early Life of Thomas Hardy,* believed to have been written largely by Hardy himself.

1930   *Collected Poems* published posthumously. Florence Emily Hardy publishes *The Later Years of Thomas Hardy.*

Contributors

HAROLD BLOOM, Sterling Professor of the Humanities at Yale University, is the author of *The Anxiety of Influence, Poetry and Repression,* and many other volumes of literary criticism. His forthcoming study, *Freud: Trans-ference and Authority,* attempts a full-scale reading of all of Freud's major writings. A MacArthur Prize Fellow, he is general editor of five series of literary criticism published by Chelsea House.

MICHAEL MILLGATE is Professor of English at the University of Toronto. In addition to his biography on Hardy, Millgate is author of *The Achieve-ment of William Faulkner.* He has also edited a book on Tennyson.

JANET BURSTEIN is Assistant Professor of English at Drew University.

IAN GREGOR is Professor of Modern English Literature at the University of Kent. He is author of several books, and has edited a collection of critical essays on the Brontës.

TERRY EAGLETON is Lecturer in English at Oxford University, and the author of many books of criticism. His most recent publications include *The Rape of Clarissa: Writing, Sexuality and Class Struggle in Richardson* and *Literary Theory: An Introduction.*

NORMAN PAGE is Professor of English at the University of Alberta. He has written several critical books, including *Thomas Hardy: The Writer and His Background, A Conrad Companion, A Dickens Com_r_nion,* and *Wilkie Collins.* He has also edited books on D. H. Lawrence, Henry James, Tennyson, and Nabokov.

KATHLEEN BLAKE is Professor of English at the University of Washington in Seattle. Her publications include *Love and the Woman Question in Vic-torian Literature: The Art of Self-Postponement* and *Play, Games, and Sport: The Literary Works of Lewis Carroll.*

RAMÓN SALDÍVAR teaches at the University of Texas at Austin. His publications include *Figural Language in the Novel: The Flowers of Speech from Cervantes to Joyce.*

PHILIP M. WEINSTEIN teaches at Swarthmore College. His most recent book is *The Semantics of Desire: The Changing Roles of Identity from Dickens to Joyce.*

Bibliography

Abercrombie, Lascelles. *Thomas Hardy: A Critical Study.* London: Martin Secker, 1912.

Bayley, John. *An Essay on Hardy.* Cambridge: Cambridge University Press, 1978.

Beach, Joseph Warren. *The Technique of Thomas Hardy.* Chicago: University of Chicago Press, 1922.

Benvenuto, Richard. "Modes of Perception: The Will to Live in *Jude the Obscure.*" *Studies in the Novel* 2 (1970): 31–41.

Bloom, Harold, ed. *Modern Critical Views: Thomas Hardy.* New Haven: Chelsea House, 1986.

Boumelha, Penny. *Thomas Hardy and Women: Sexual Ideology and Narrative Form.* Brighton, Sussex: Harvester, 1982.

Brooks, Jean R. *Thomas Hardy: The Poetic Structure.* London: Elek Books, 1971.

Brown, Douglas. *Thomas Hardy.* 1954. Reprint. Westport, Conn.: Greenwood, 1980.

Burns, Wayne. "Flesh and Spirit in *Jude the Obscure.*" *Recovering Literature* 1 (1972): 26–41.

Carpenter, Richard. *Thomas Hardy.* New York: Twayne, 1964.

Casagrande, Peter J. *Unity in Hardy's Novels.* Lawrence, Kans.: The Regents Press of Kansas, 1982.

Cecil, David. *Hardy the Novelist.* New York: Bobbs-Merrill, 1946.

Chew, Samuel C. *Thomas Hardy: Poet and Novelist.* Second revision. New York: Russell & Russell, 1964.

Childers, Mary. "Thomas Hardy, The Man Who 'Liked' Women." *Criticism* 23, no. 4 (1981): 317–34.

Cockshut, A. O. J. *Man and Woman: A Study of Love and the Novel 1740–1940.* London: Collins, 1977.

Cox, R. G., ed. *Thomas Hardy: The Critical Heritage.* London: Routledge & Kegan Paul, 1970.

Daiches, David. *Some Late Victorian Attitudes.* New York: Norton, 1969.

DeLaura, David. "The Ache of Modernism in Hardy's Later Novels." *ELH* 34, no. 3 (1967): 380–99.

Drabble, Margaret, ed. *The Genius of Thomas Hardy.* New York: Knopf, 1976.

Draper, Ronald P., ed. *Hardy: The Tragic Novels, A Casebook.* London: Macmillan, 1975.

Emmett, V. J., Jr. "Marriage in Hardy's Later Novels." *Midwest Quarterly* 10 (1969): 331–48.

Fischler, Alexander. "An Affinity for Birds: Kindness in Hardy's *Jude the Obscure*." *Studies in the Novel* 13 (1981): 250–65.

Gerber, Helmut E., and W. Eugene Davis, eds. *Thomas Hardy: An Annotated Bibliography of Writings about Him*. De Kalb: Northern Illinois University Press, 1973.

Giordano, Frank R., Jr. "*Jude the Obscure* and the *Bildungsroman*." *Studies in the Novel* 4 (1972): 580–91.

Gittings, Robert. *Young Thomas Hardy*. Boston: Little, Brown, 1975.

Goetz, William R. "The Felicity and Infelicity of Marriage in *Jude the Obscure*." *Nineteenth-Century Fiction* 38 (1983): 189–213.

Guerard, Albert J. *Thomas Hardy: The Novels and Stories*. Cambridge: Harvard University Press, 1949.

———, ed. *Hardy: A Collection of Critical Essays*. Englewood Cliffs, N.J.: Prentice-Hall, 1963.

Hardy, Evelyn. *Thomas Hardy: A Critical Biography*. London: Hogarth, 1954.

Hardy, Florence Emily. *The Life of Thomas Hardy, 1840–1928*. London: Macmillan, 1962. Reprint. Hamden, Conn.: Shoe String Press, 1970.

Hassett, E. "Compromised Romanticism in *Jude the Obscure*." *Nineteenth-Century Fiction* 25 (1971): 432–43.

Hawkins, Desmond. *Thomas Hardy*. Darby, Pa.: Folcroft Library Editions, 1950.

Heilman, Robert B. "Hardy's Sue Bridehead." *Nineteenth-Century Fiction* 20 (1966): 307–23.

Hornback, Bert A. *The Metaphor of Chance: Vision and Technique in the Works of Thomas Hardy*. Athens: Ohio University Press, 1971.

Horne, Lewis B. "Pattern and Contrast in *Jude the Obscure*." *Études Anglaises* 2 (April–June 1979): 143–53.

Howe, Irving. *Thomas Hardy*. New York: Macmillan, 1967.

Hyman, Virginia R. *Ethical Perspective in the Novels of Thomas Hardy*. Port Washington, N.Y.: Kennikat, 1975.

Ingham, Patricia. "The Evolution of *Jude the Obscure*." *The Review of English Studies* 27 (1976): 27–37, 159–69.

Jacobus, Mary. "Sue the Obscure." *Essays in Criticism* 25, no. 3 (1975): 304–28.

Johnson, Bruce. *True Correspondence: A Phenomenology of Thomas Hardy's Novels*. Tallahassee: University Presses of Florida, 1983.

Johnson, Lionel. *The Art of Thomas Hardy*. New York: Russell & Russell, 1965.

Knoepflmacher, U. C. *Laughter and Despair in Ten Novels of the Victorian Era*. Berkeley: University of California Press, 1971.

Kramer, Dale. *Thomas Hardy: The Forms of Tragedy*. Detroit: Wayne State University Press, 1975.

Langlund, Elizabeth. "A Perspective of One's Own: Thomas Hardy and the Elusive Sue Bridehead." *Studies in the Novel* 12 (1980): 12–28.

Lawrence, D. H. *Phoenix: The Posthumous Papers of D. H. Lawrence*. New York: Viking, 1972.

Lerner, Laurence, and John Holstrom, eds. *Thomas Hardy and His Readers: A Selection of Contemporary Reviews*. New York: Barnes & Noble, 1968.

Lodge, David. "*Jude the Obscure*: Pessimism and Fictional Form." In *Critical Ap-*

proaches to the Fiction of Thomas Hardy, edited by Dale Kramer. London: Macmillan, 1979.

McDowell, Frederick P. W. "Hardy's 'Seemings or Personal Impressions': The Symbolical Use of Image and Contrast in *Jude the Obscure.*" *Modern Fiction Studies* 6 (1960): 233–50.

Meisel, Perry. *Thomas Hardy: The Return of the Repressed.* New Haven and London: Yale University Press, 1972.

Miller, J. Hillis. *Thomas Hardy: Distance and Desire.* Cambridge: Harvard University Press, 1970.

Millgate, Michael. *Thomas Hardy: A Biography.* New York: Random House, 1982.

Millgate, Michael, and Richard Little Purdy, eds. *The Collected Letters of Thomas Hardy.* 3 volumes to date. Oxford University Press, 1978–.

Mizener, Arthur. "*Jude the Obscure* as a Tragedy." *The Southern Review* 6 (1940–41): 193–213.

Morrell, Roy. *Thomas Hardy: The Will and the Way.* Kuala Lumpur: University of Malaya Press, 1968.

———. "Thomas Hardy and Probability." In *On the Novel: A Present for Walter Allen on His Sixtieth Birthday from His Friends and Colleagues,* edited by B. S. Bededikz, 75–92. London: J. M. Dent, 1971.

Paterson, John. "The Genesis of *Jude the Obscure.*" *Studies in Philology* 57 (1960): 87–98.

Pinion, F. B., ed. *A Hardy Companion: A Guide to the Works of Thomas Hardy and Their Background.* New York: St. Martin's, 1968.

———. *Thomas Hardy and the Modern World.* Dorchester, Dorset: Thomas Hardy Society, 1974.

Rachman, Shalom. "Character and Theme in Hardy's *Jude the Obscure.*" *English* 22, no. 113 (1973): 45–53.

Schwarz, Barry N. "*Jude the Obscure* in the Age of Anxiety." *Studies in English Literature 1500–1900* 10, no. 4 (1970): 793–804.

Smith, Anne. *The Novels of Thomas Hardy.* London: Vision Press, 1979.

Sonstroem, David. "Order and Disorder in *Jude the Obscure.*" *English Literature in Transition (1880–1920)* 24, no. 1 (1981): 6–15.

Starzyk, Lawrence J. "The Coming Universal Wish Not to Live in Hardy's 'Modern' Novels." *Nineteenth-Century Fiction* 26 (1972): 419–35.

Steig, Michael. "Sue Bridehead." *Novel* 1 (1968): 260–66.

Stewart, J. I. M. *Thomas Hardy: A Critical Biography.* New York: Dodd, Mead, 1971.

Thomas Hardy Annual, 1983–.

The Thomas Hardy Society Review, 1975–.

The Thomas Hardy Yearbook, 1970–.

Thurley, Geoffrey. *The Psychology of Hardy's Novels.* Queensland: University of Queensland Press, 1975.

Woolf, Virginia. *The Second Common Reader.* New York: Harcourt, Brace, 1950.

Zabel, Morton Dauwen. "Hardy in Defense of His Art: The Aesthetic of Incongruity." *The Southern Review* 6 (1940–41): 125–49.

Acknowledgments

"The Tragedy of Unfulfilled Aims" (originally entitled "*Jude the Obscure*") by Michael Millgate from *Thomas Hardy: His Career as a Novelist* by Michael Millgate, © 1971 by Michael Millgate. Reprinted by permission of Random House, Inc., and A D Peters & Co. Ltd.

"The Journey beyond Myth in *Jude the Obscure*" by Janet Burstein from *Texas Studies in Literature and Language* 15, no. 3 (Fall 1973), © 1973 by the University of Texas Press. Reprinted by permission of the author and the University of Texas Press.

"An End and a Beginning: *Jude the Obscure*" by Ian Gregor from *The Great Web: The Form of Hardy's Major Fiction* by Ian Gregor, © 1974 by Ian Gregor. Reprinted by permission of Faber & Faber Ltd.

"The Limits of Art" (originally entitled "Introduction") by Terry Eagleton from *Jude the Obscure,* edited by Terry Eagleton, © 1974 by Macmillan Publishers Ltd. Reprinted by permission.

"Vision and Blindness" (originally entitled "Major Novels") by Norman Page from *Thomas Hardy* by Norman Page, © 1977 by Norman Page. Reprinted by permission of Routledge & Kegan Paul.

"Sue Bridehead, 'The Woman of the Feminist Movement'" by Kathleen Blake from *Studies in English Literature 1500–1900* 18, no. 4 (Autumn 1978), © 1978 by William Marsh Rice University. Reprinted by permission.

"*Jude the Obscure:* Reading and the Spirit of the Law" by Ramón Saldívar from *ELH* 50, no. 3 (1983), © 1983 by the Johns Hopkins University Press. Reprinted by permission of the Johns Hopkins University Press.

"'The Spirit Unappeased and Peregrine': *Jude the Obscure*" by Philip M. Weinstein from *The Semantics of Desire: Changing Models of Identity from Dickens to Joyce* by Philip M. Weinstein, © 1984 by Princeton University Press. Reprinted by permission of Princeton University Press.

Index